Grade 1

Your Turn
Practice Book

Mc
Graw
Hill
Education

Contents

Start Smart

Week One

Phonics: /m/m, /s/s SS1
Phonics: /a/a SS2
Smart Start Reader: *I Like To* SS3
Handwriting: *Mm, Ss, Aa* SS5
Phonics: /p/p, /t/t SS6
Phonics: /r/r, /n/n SS7
Handwriting: *Pp, Tt, Nn* SS8
Smart Start Reader: *He Can Go!* SS9
Phonics: /i/i SS11
Handwriting: *Rr, Ii* SS12

Week Two

Phonics: /k/c, /f/f SS13
Phonics: /o/o SS14
Smart Start Reader: *Look!* SS15
Handwriting: *Cc, Ff, Oo* SS17
Phonics: /d/d, /h/h SS18
Phonics: /e/e SS19
Handwriting: *Dd, Hh, Ee* SS20
Smart Start Reader: *We Play Here* SS21
Phonics: /b/b, /l/l SS23
Handwriting: *Bb, Ll* SS24

Week Three

Phonics: /k/k, /k/ck SS25
Phonics: /u/u SS26
Smart Start Reader: *With Me* SS27
Handwriting: *Kk, Uu, Gg* SS29
Phonics: /g/g, /w/w SS30
Phonics: /kw/q, /v/v, /ks/x SS31
Handwriting: *Ww, Xx, Vv* SS32
Start Smart Reader: *He and She Go* . . . SS33
Phonics: /j/j, /y/y, /z/z SS35
Handwriting: *Qq, Jj, Yy, Zz* SS36

Contents

Unit I • Getting to Know Us

Week I

At School

Phonics: Short *a* I

High-Frequency Words 2

Phonics: Short *a* 3

Comprehension: Key Details Chart 4

Comprehension: Mini Book
Jack the Cat 5

Comprehension: Story Questions
Key Details 7

Structural Analysis: Inflectional Ending *-s* . . 8

Text Feature: Photographs 9

Writing Trait: Ideas 10

Week 2

Where I Live

Phonics: Short *i* II

High-Frequency Words 12

Phonics: Short *i* 13

Comprehension: Key Details Chart 14

Comprehension: Mini Book
Pip and Tip 15

Comprehension: Story Questions
Key Details 17

Structural Analysis: Double
Final Consonants 18

Text Feature: Bold Print 19

Writing Trait: Ideas 20

Week 3

Our Pets

Phonics: *l*-Blends 21

High-Frequency Words 22

Phonics: *l*-Blends 23

Comprehension: Key Details Chart 24

Comprehension: Mini Book
Kim and Flick 25

Comprehension: Story Questions
Key Details 27

Structural Analysis: Plural Nouns 28

Text Feature: Labels 29

Writing Trait: Ideas 30

Week 4

Let's Be Friends

Phonics: Short *o* 31

High-Frequency Words 32

Phonics: Short *o* 33

Comprehension: Key Details Chart 34

Comprehension: Mini Book
What Can It Do? 35

Comprehension: Story Questions
Key Details 37

Structural Analysis: Alphabetical Order . . 38

Literary Element: Rhyme 39

Writing Trait: Organization 40

Week 5

Let's Move!

Phonics: *r*-Blends and *s*-Blends 41

High-Frequency Words 42

Phonics: *r*-Blends and *s*-Blends 43

Comprehension: Key Details Chart 44

Comprehension: Mini Book
Kids Can Move 45

Comprehension: Story Questions
Key Details 47

Structural Analysis: Possessives 48

Text Feature: Diagram 49

Writing Trait: Organization 50

Unit 2 · Our Community

Week 1

Jobs Around Town

Phonics: Short *e* 51

High-Frequency Words 52

Phonics: Short *e* 53

Comprehension: Character,
Setting, Events Chart. 54

Comprehension: Mini Book
A Fun Job. 55

Comprehension: Story Questions
Character, Setting, Events 57

Structural Analysis: Inflectional
Ending *-ed* 58

Text Feature: Labels. 59

Writing Trait: Organization 60

Week 2

Buildings All Around

Phonics: Short *u* 61

High-Frequency Words 62

Phonics: Short *u* 63

Comprehension: Character, Setting,
Events Chart 64

Comprehension: Mini Book
Pals Play and Hum 65

Comprehension: Story Questions
Character, Setting, Events 67

Structural Analysis: Contractions with *'s* . . 68

Text Feature: Captions. 69

Writing Trait: Organization 70

Week 3

A Community in Nature

Phonics: End Blends 71

High-Frequency Words 72

Phonics: End Blends 73

Comprehension: Main Topic and
Details Chart. 74

Comprehension: Mini Book
Big Rock Pond 75

Comprehension: Story Questions
Main Topic and Key Details 77

Structural Analysis: Inflectional
Ending *-ing*. 78

Literary Element: Repetition. 79

Writing Trait: Ideas 80

Week 4

Let's Help

Phonics: Consonant Digraphs *sh, th, -ng* . . . 81

High-Frequency Words 82

Phonics: Consonant Digraphs *sh, th, -ng* . . . 83

Comprehension: Character, Setting,
Events Chart 84

Comprehension: Mini Book
All Help with the Play 85

Comprehension: Story Questions
Character, Setting, Events 87

Structural Analysis: Closed Syllables. 88

Text Feature: List 89

Writing Trait: Organization 90

Week 5

Follow the Map

Phonics: Consonant Digraphs *ch, -tch,
wh, ph*. 91

High-Frequency Words 92

Phonics: Consonant Digraphs *ch,
-tch, wh, ph* 93

Comprehension: Main Topic and
Details Chart. 94

Comprehension: Mini Book
Look Around 95

Comprehension: Story Questions
Main Topic and Key Details 97

Structural Analysis: Inflectional
Ending *-es* 98

Text Feature: Map 99

Writing Trait: Ideas 100

Contents

Unit 3 • Changes Over Time

Week 1

What Time Is It?

Phonics: Long *a: a_e* 101

High-Frequency Words 102

Phonics: Long *a: a_e* 103

Comprehension: Sequence Chart 104

Comprehension: Mini Book
Whale at the Lake. 105

Comprehension: Story Questions
Character, Setting, Plot 107

Structural Analysis: Contractions
with *not* 108

Text Feature: Bold Print. 109

Writing Trait: Word Choice 110

Week 2

Watch It Grow!

Phonics: Long *i: i_e* 111

High-Frequency Words 112

Phonics: Long *i: i_e* 113

Comprehension: Sequence Chart 114

Comprehension: Mini Book
A Gift for Mom 115

Comprehension: Story Questions
Sequence 117

Structural Analysis: Plurals 118

Text Feature: Diagrams. 119

Writing Trait: Word Choice 120

Week 3

Tales Over Time

Phonics: Soft *c*, Soft *g*, *dge*. 121

High-Frequency Words 122

Phonics: Soft *c*, Soft *g*, *dge*. 123

Comprehension: Cause and Effect Chart . . 124

Comprehension: Mini Book
Little Fred and Little Buck 125

Comprehension: Story Questions
Cause and Effect 127

Structural Analysis: Inflectional
Endings *-ed* and *-ing* (drop final *e*) 128

Literary Element: Rhyme 129

Writing Trait: Word Choice 130

Week 4

Now and Then

Phonics: /ō/*o_e*, /ū/*u_e*, /ē/*e_e* 131

High-Frequency Words 132

Phonics: /ō/*o_e*, /ū/*u_e*, /ē/*e_e* 133

Comprehension: Compare and
Contrast Chart 134

Comprehension: Mini Book
Life Long Ago 135

Comprehension: Story Questions
Compare and Contrast 137

Structural Analysis: CVCe Syllables 138

Text Feature: Captions. 139

Writing Trait: Ideas 140

Week 5

From Farm to Table

Phonics: /ù/ *oo, u* 141

High-Frequency Words 142

Phonics: /ù/ *oo, u* 143

Comprehension: Sequence Chart 144

Comprehension: Mini Book
The Food We Eat 145

Comprehension: Story Questions
Sequence 147

Structural Analysis: Inflectional
Endings *-ed*, *-ing*. 148

Text Feature: Chart 149

Writing Trait: Ideas 150

Unit 4 · Animals Everywhere

Week 1
Animal Features
Phonics: Long *a: a, ai, ay* 151
High-Frequency Words 152
Vocabulary: *special, splendid*. 153
Comprehension: Sequence Chart 154
Comprehension: Mini Book
A Fox Tail 155
Comprehension: Story Questions
Plot: Sequence 157
Vocabulary Strategy: Use a Dictionary. . . 158
Phonics: Long *a: a, ai, ay* 159
Structural Analysis: Alphabetical Order . . 160
Text Feature: Chart 161
Writing Trait: Word Choice 162

Week 2
Animals Together
Phonics: Long *e: e, ea, ee, ie* 163
High-Frequency Words 164
Vocabulary: *danger, partner* 165
Comprehension: Main Idea and
Key Details Chart 166
Comprehension: Mini Book
Ants Can Help 167
Comprehension: Story Questions
Main Idea and Key Details 169
Vocabulary Strategy: Context Clues –
Sentence Clues 170
Phonics: Long *e: e, ea, ee, ie* 171
Structural Analysis: Prefixes: *re-,
un-, pre-* 172
Text Feature: Captions. 173
Writing Trait: Organization 174

Week 3
In the Wild
Phonics: Long *o: o, oa, ow, oe* 175
High-Frequency Words 176
Vocabulary: *seek, search* 177
Comprehension: Main Idea and
Key Details Chart 178

Comprehension: Mini Book *Crows* 179
Comprehension: Story Questions
Main Idea and Key Details. 181
Vocabulary Strategy: Word Categories . . 182
Phonics: Long *o: o, oa, ow, oe* 183
Structural Analysis: Open Syllables 184
Literary Element: Sensory Words 185
Writing Trait: Organization 186

Week 4
Insects!
Phonics: Long *i: i, y, igh, ie* 187
High-Frequency Words 188
Vocabulary: *beautiful, fancy* 189
Comprehension: Point of View Chart . . . 190
Comprehension: Mini Book
Eve and Pete .191
Comprehension: Story Questions
Point of View. 193
Vocabulary Strategy: Context Clues. . . . 194
Phonics: Long *i: i, y, igh, ie* 195
Structural Analysis: Inflectional
Endings (change *y* to *i*) 196
Text Feature: Headings 197
Writing Trait: Organization 198

Week 5
Working with Animals
Phonics: Long *e: y, ey*. 199
High-Frequency Words 200
Vocabulary: *clever, signal*. 201
Comprehension: Sequence Chart 202
Comprehension: Mini Book
A New Puppy. 203
Comprehension: Story Questions
Sequence 205
Vocabulary Strategy: Root Words. 206
Phonics: Long *e: y, ey*. 207
Structural Analysis: Compound Words . . .208
Text Feature: Captions. 209
Writing Trait: Word Choice 210

Contents

Unit 5 · Figure It Out

Week 1
See It, Sort It
Phonics: /är/ar 211

High-Frequency Words 212

Vocabulary: *trouble, whole* 213

Comprehension: Point of View Chart . . 214

Comprehension: Mini Book
The Party 215

Comprehension: Story Questions
Point of View 217

Vocabulary Strategy: Context Clues –
Multiple Meaning Words 218

Phonics: /är/ar 219

Structural Analysis: Irregular Plurals . . . 220

Text Feature: Use Photographs/
Illustrations 221

Writing Trait: Sentence Fluency 222

Week 2
Up in the Sky
Phonics: /ûr/er, ir, ur, or 223

High-Frequency Words 224

Vocabulary: *leaped, stretched* 225

Comprehension: Cause and Effect Chart . . .226

Comprehension: Mini Book
A Bunny Wish 227

Comprehension: Story Questions
Cause and Effect 229

Vocabulary Strategy: Shades of Meaning . . 230

Phonics: /ûr/er, ir, ur, or 231

Structural Analysis: Inflectional Ending -er . . 232

Text Feature: Captions 233

Writing Trait: Word Choice 234

Week 3
Great Inventions
Phonics: /ôr/or, ore, oar 235

High-Frequency Words 236

Vocabulary: *idea, unusual* 237

Comprehension: Problem and
Solution Chart 238

Comprehension: Mini Book
Good Ideas 239

Comprehension: Story Questions
Problem and Solution 241

Vocabulary Strategy: Prefixes 242

Phonics: /ôr/or, ore, oar 243

Structural Analysis: Abbreviations 244

Literary Element: Alliteration 245

Writing Trait: Word Choice 246

Week 4
Sounds All Around
Phonics: Diphthongs *ou, ow* 247

High-Frequency Words 248

Vocabulary: *scrambled, suddenly* 249

Comprehension: Problem and Solution
Chart 250

Comprehension: Mini Book
Dad's Game 251

Comprehension: Story Questions
Plot: Problem and Solution 253

Vocabulary Strategy: Suffixes 254

Phonics: Diphthongs *ou, ow* 255

Structural Analysis: Inflectional
Endings -er, -est 256

Text Feature: Directions 257

Writing Trait: Sentence Fluency 258

Week 5
Build It!
Phonics: Diphthongs *oi, oy* 259

High-Frequency Words 260

Vocabulary: *balance, section* 261

Comprehension: Cause and Effect Chart . . . 262

Comprehension: Mini Book
How to Build a Snowman 263

Comprehension: Story Questions
Cause and Effect 265

Vocabulary Strategy: Inflectional Endings . . 266

Phonics: Diphthongs *oi, oy* 267

Structural Analysis:
Final Stable Syllables 268

Text Feature: Captions 269

Writing Trait: Organization 270

Unit 6 · Together We Can!

Week I
Taking Action
Phonics: Variant Vowel /ü/ 271
High-Frequency Words 272
Vocabulary: *demand, emergency* 273
Comprehension: Theme Chart 274
Comprehension: Mini Book
   Working Together 275
Comprehension: Story Questions
   Theme 277
Vocabulary Strategy: Synonyms 278
Phonics: Variant Vowel /ü/ 279
Structural Analysis: Suffixes *-ful, -less* . . 280
Text Feature: Captions 281
Writing Trait: Sentence Fluency 282

Week 2
My Team
Phonics: Variant Vowel /ô/ 283
High-Frequency Words 284
Vocabulary: *accept, often* 285
Comprehension: Author's Purpose Chart . . .286
Comprehension: Mini Book
   Coaches 287
Comprehension: Story Questions
   Author's Purpose 289
Vocabulary Strategy: Antonyms 290
Phonics: Variant Vowel /ô/ 291
Structural Analysis: Vowel-Team Syllables . .292
Literary Element: Sensory Words 293
Writing Trait: Voice 294

Week 3
Weather Together
Phonics: Silent Letters *wr, kn, gn* 295
High-Frequency Words 296
Vocabulary: *country, gathers* 297
Comprehension: Cause and Effect Chart . . . 298
Comprehension: Mini Book
   Storm Watch 299

Comprehension: Story Questions
   Plot: Cause and Effect 301
Vocabulary Strategy: Similes 302
Phonics: Silent Letters *wr, kn, gn* 303
Structural Analysis: Compound Words . . .304
Text Feature: Headings 305
Writing Trait: Ideas 306

Week 4
Sharing Traditions
Phonics: Three-Letter Blends 307
High-Frequency Words 308
Vocabulary: *difficult, nobody* 309
Comprehension: Theme Chart 310
Comprehension: Mini Book
   Sue's Surprise .311
Comprehension: Story Questions
   Theme 313
Vocabulary Strategy: Compound Words . . . 314
Phonics: Three-Letter Blends 315
Structural Analysis: Inflectional
Endings *-ed, -ing* 316
Text Feature: Directions 317
Writing Trait: Sentence Fluency 318

Week 5
Celebrate America!
Phonics: /âr/*air, are, ear* 319
High-Frequency Words 320
Vocabulary: *nation, unite* 321
Comprehension: Author's Purpose Chart . .322
Comprehension: Mini Book
   Favorite Days .323
Comprehension: Story Questions
   Author's Purpose 325
Vocabulary Strategy: Metaphors 326
Phonics: /âr/*air, are, ear* 327
Structural Analysis: *r*-Controlled Vowel
   Syllables 328
Text Feature: Map 329
Writing Trait: Voice 330

Name _____

A. Say each picture name. Write <u>m</u> below the picture if its name begins like <u>map</u>. Write <u>s</u> if its name begins like <u>sun</u>.

B. Say each picture name. Then write <u>m</u> below the picture if its name ends like <u>jam</u>.

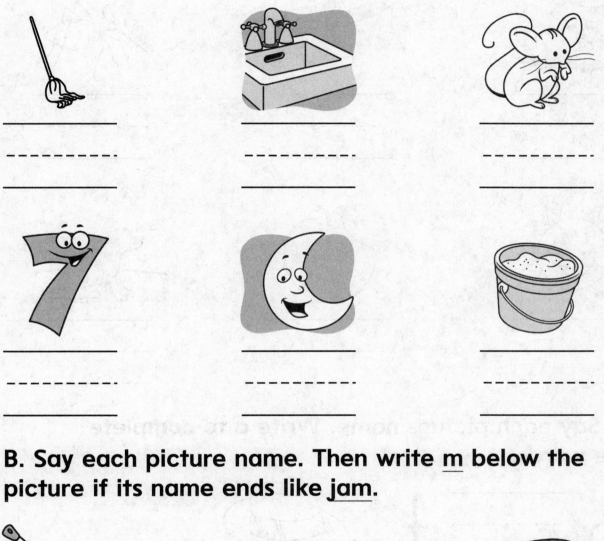

Name _____

A. Say each picture name. Write <u>a</u> below the picture if its name begins with <u>a</u> as in <u>apple</u>.

----------   ----------   ----------

----------   ----------   ----------

B. Say each picture name. Write <u>a</u> to complete the words.

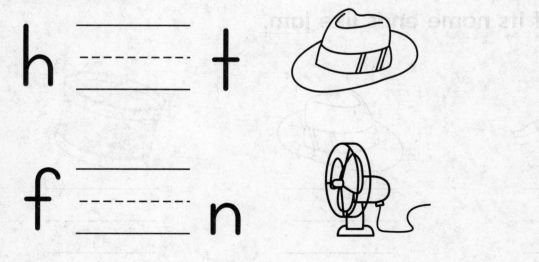

(4)

Do you?

High-Frequency Words: do, I, like, to, you

I Like To

I like to
.

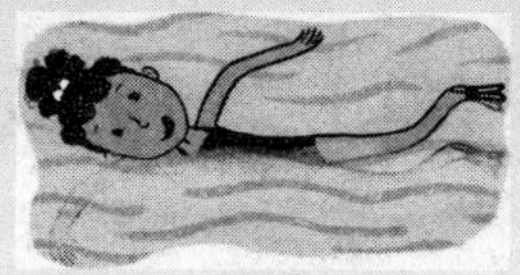

(1)

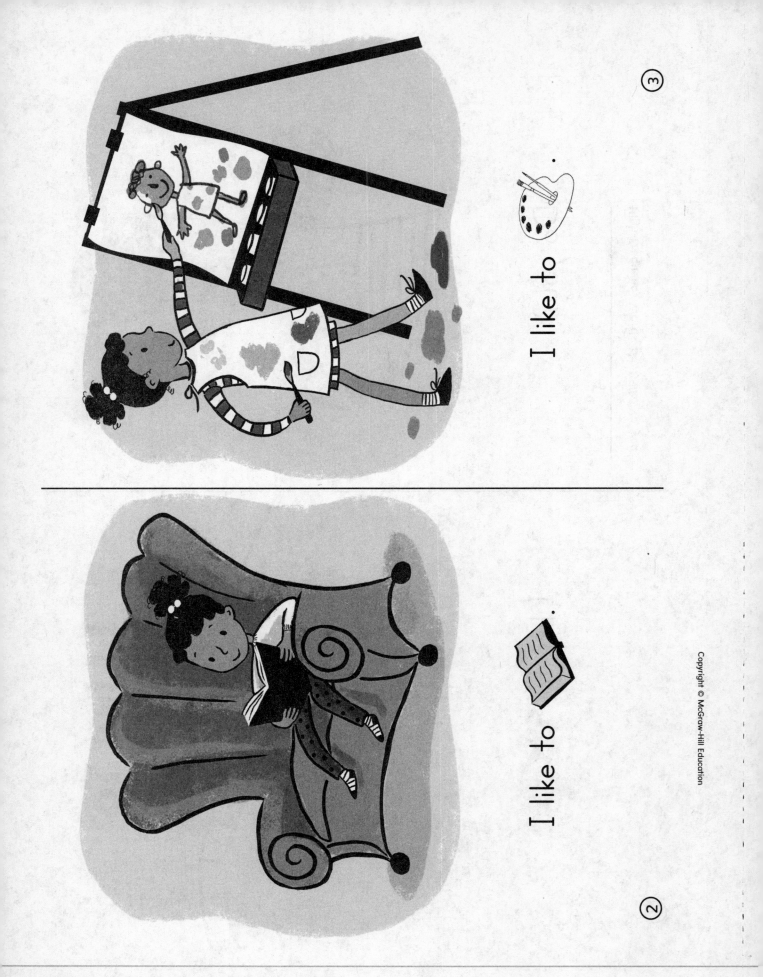

I like to ____ .

③

I like to ____ .

②

Name _____

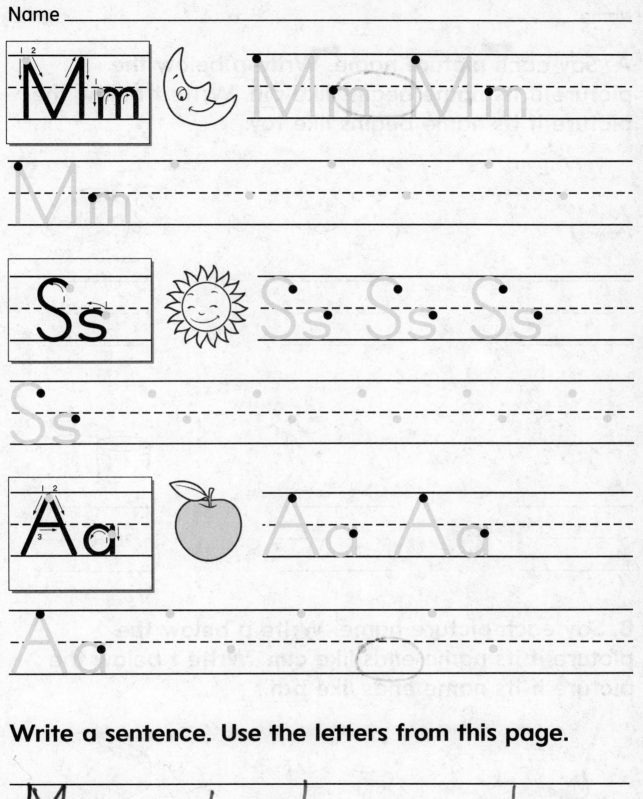

Write a sentence. Use the letters from this page.

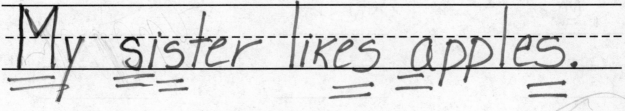

My sister likes apples.

Name _____

A. Say each picture name. Write <u>p</u> below the picture if its name (begins) like <u>pin</u>. Write <u>t</u> below the picture if its name begins like <u>toy</u>.

_____
- - - - - - - - - -
_____

_____
- - - - - - - - - -
_____

_____
- - - - - - - - - -
_____

_____
- - - - - - - - - -
_____

_____
- - - - - - - - - -
_____

_____
- - - - - - - - - -
_____

B. Say each picture name. Write <u>p</u> below the picture if its name (ends) like <u>cup</u>. Write <u>t</u> below the picture if its name ends like <u>bat</u>.

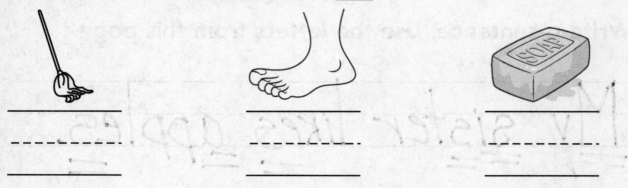

Name _____

A. Say each picture name. Write <u>n</u> below the picture if its name begins like <u>nest</u>. Write <u>r</u> if its name begins like <u>rat</u>.

_ _ _ _ _ _ _ _ _

_ _ _ _ _ _ _ _ _

_ _ _ _ _ _ _ _ _

_ _ _ _ _ _ _ _ _

_ _ _ _ _ _ _ _ _

_ _ _ _ _ _ _ _ _

B. Say each picture name. Then write <u>n</u> below the picture if its name ends like <u>fun</u>.

_ _

Name _____

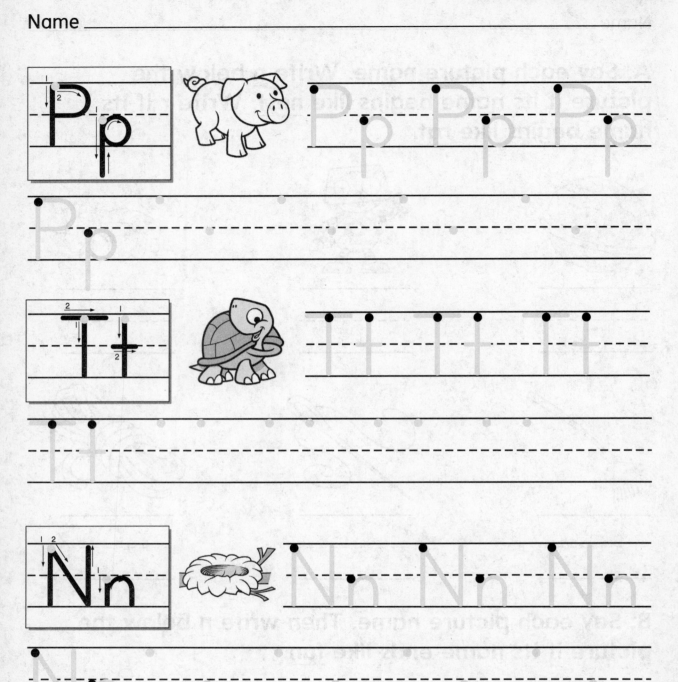

Write a sentence. Use the letters from this page.

_____

- -

_____

He can go!

High-Frequency Words: a, can, go, has, he

He has a 🧤.

He Can Go!

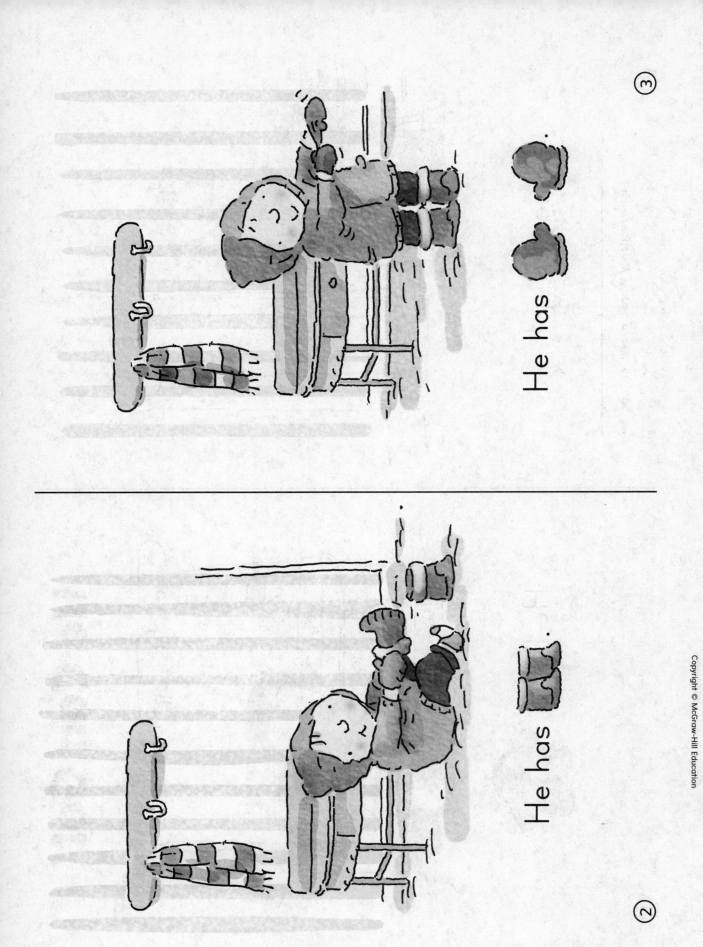

He has ____.

He has ____.

Name _____

A. Say each picture name. Write i below the picture if its name begins with i as in ink.

B. Say each picture name. Write i to complete the words.

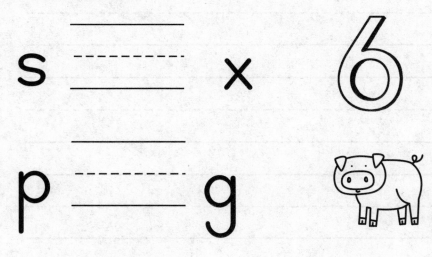

Name _____

Write some sentences. Use the letters from this page.

_____

- -

_____

- -

_____

- -

_____

- -

_____

Name _____

A. Say each picture name. Write c below the picture if its name begins like cat. Write f if its name begins like fun.

_____   _____   _____

- - - - -   - - - - -   - - - - -

_____   _____   _____

- - - - -   - - - - -   - - - - -

B. Say each picture name. Write c or f to complete the words.

_____ a t

- - - - -

_____ a n

- - - - -

Name _____

A. Say each picture name. Write o below the picture if its name begins with o as in ox.

_____   _____   _____
- - - - - - - - -   - - - - - - - - -   - - - - - - - - -
_____   _____   _____

_____   _____   _____
- - - - - - - - -   - - - - - - - - -   - - - - - - - - -
_____   _____   _____

B. Say each picture name. Write o to complete the words.

_____
- - - - - - - -   x
_____

b - - - - - - - -   x
_____

High-Frequency Words: *is, look, little, my, this*

This is my _____!

Look!

Look! This is my _____.

Look! This is my little ___.

③

Look! This is my ___.

②

Name _____

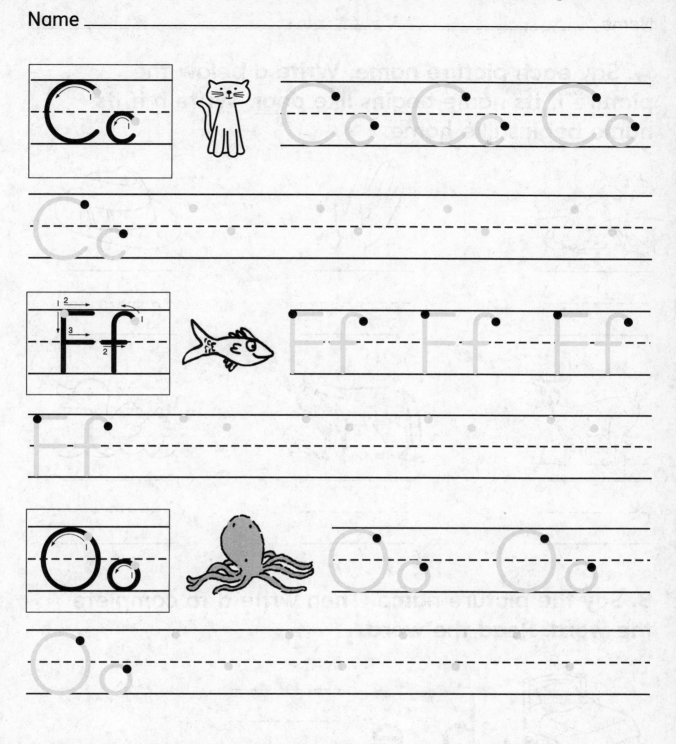

Write a sentence. Use the letters from this page.

_____

- -

_____

Name _____

A. Say each picture name. Write d below the picture if its name begins like <u>door</u>. Write h if its name begins like <u>home</u>.

B. Say the picture name. Then write d to complete the word. Read the word.

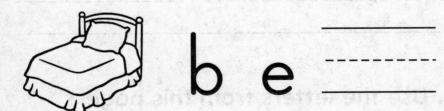

be _____

Name _____

A. Say each picture name. Write <u>e</u> below the picture if its name begins with <u>e</u> as in <u>egg</u>.

B. Say the picture name. Then write <u>e</u> to complete the word. Read the word.

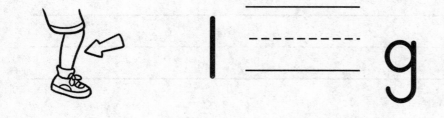

l _____ g

Name _____

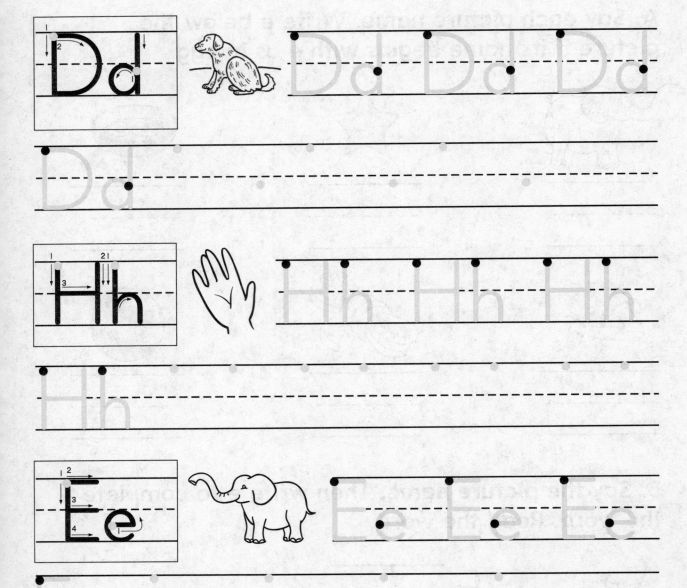

Write a sentence. Use the letters from this page.

_____

- - - - - - - - - - - - - - - -

_____

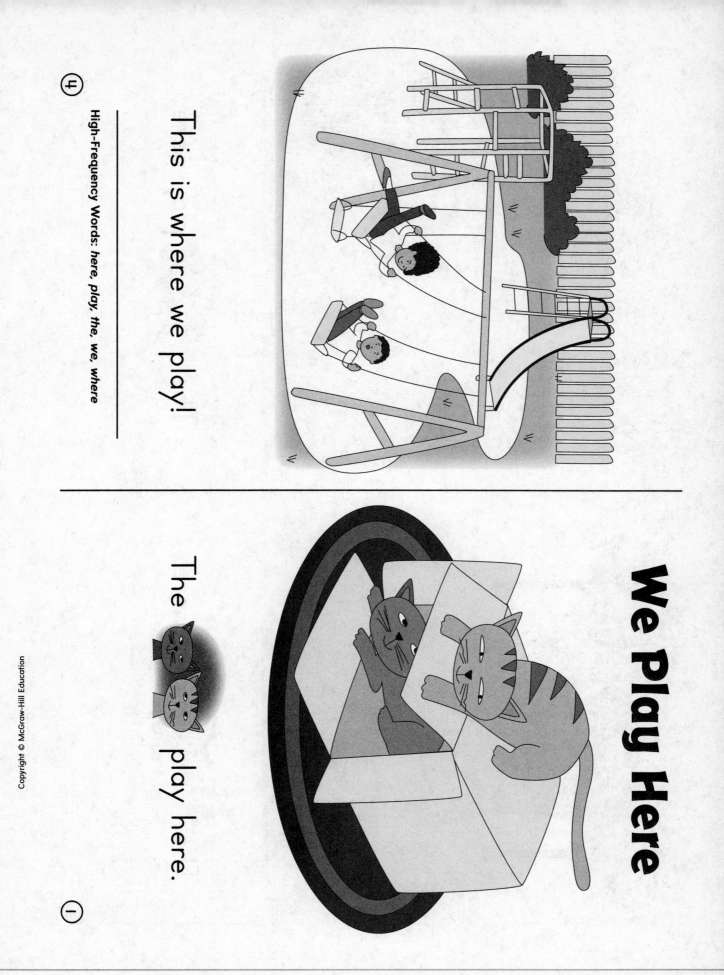

This is where we play!

High-Frequency Words: *here, play, the, we, where*

We Play Here

The ___ play here.

①

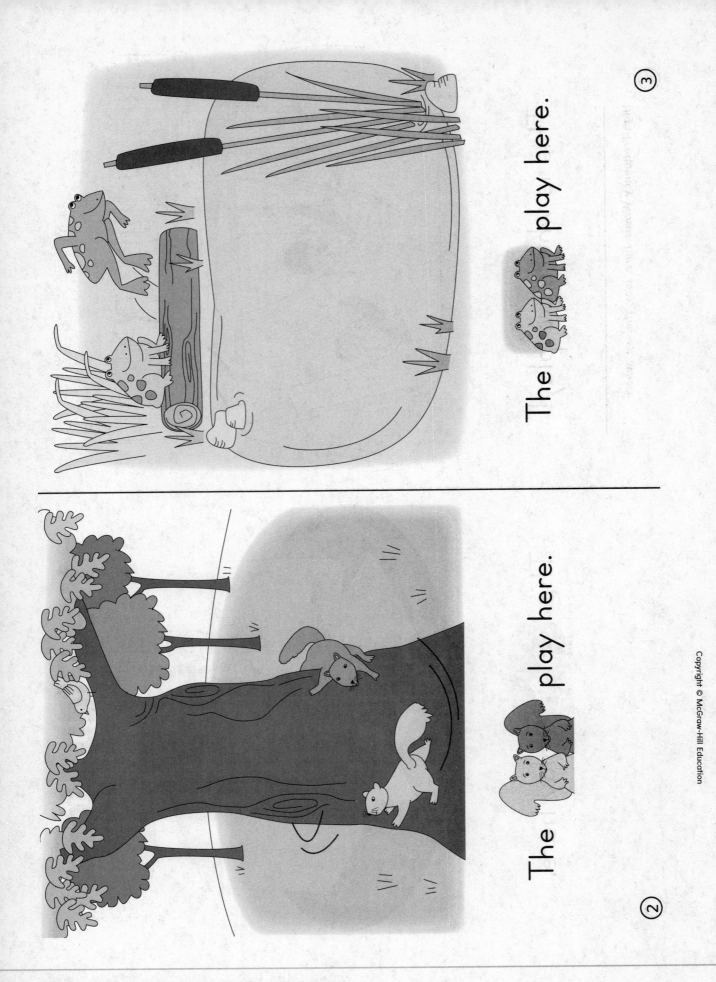

The _____ play here.

③

The _____ play here.

②

Name _____

A. Say each picture name. Write b below the picture if its name begins like bat. Write l if its name begins like lemon.

_____   _____   _____
- - - - - - - - -   - - - - - - - - -   - - - - - - - - -
_____   _____   _____

_____   _____   _____
- - - - - - - - -   - - - - - - - - -   - - - - - - - - -
_____   _____   _____

B. Say the picture name. Then write b to complete the word. Read the word.

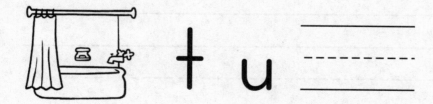 t u _____
- - - - - - - - -
_____

Name _____

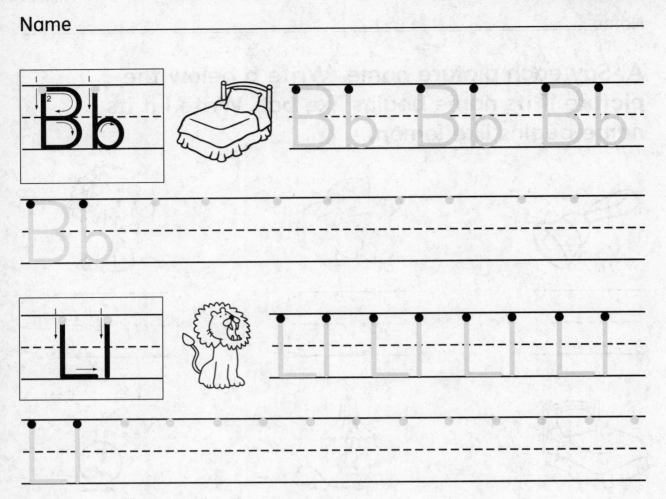

Write some sentences. Use the letters from this page.

Name _____

A. Say each picture name. Write <u>k</u> below the picture if its name begins like <u>king</u>.

_____   _____   _____

- - - - - - - - - -   - - - - - - - - - -   - - - - - - - - - -

_____   _____   _____

B. Say each picture name. Write <u>ck</u> below the picture if its name ends like <u>back</u>.

_____   _____   _____

- - - - - - - - - -   - - - - - - - - - -   - - - - - - - - - -

_____   _____   _____

C. Write the letters <u>ck</u> to make new words.

ki _____   so _____
- - - - - - - - - -   - - - - - - - - - -
_____   _____

Name _____

A. Say each picture name. Write <u>u</u> below the picture if its name begins with <u>u</u> as in <u>up</u>.

-----------	-----------	-----------

-----------	-----------	-----------

B. Say the picture name. Then write <u>u</u> to complete the word. Read the word.

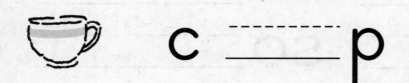

c _ _ _ _ _ _ p

High-Frequency Words: *are, for, me, she, with*

She has a ⚽ for me!

With Me

Look! I can go.

We are here.

③

She is with me.

②

Name _____

Write a sentence. Use the letters from this page.

_____

- -

_____

Name _____

A. Say each picture name. Write g below the picture if its name begins like gate. Write w if its name begins like water.

B. Say each picture name. Then write g below the picture if its name ends like dog.

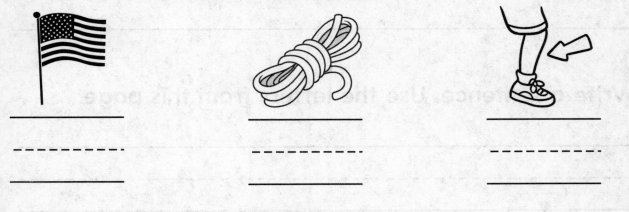

Name _____

A. Say each picture name. Write <u>q</u> below the picture if its name begins like <u>quick</u>. Write <u>v</u> if its name begins like <u>van</u>.

B. Say each picture name. Then write <u>x</u> below the picture if its name ends like <u>fox</u>.

Name _____

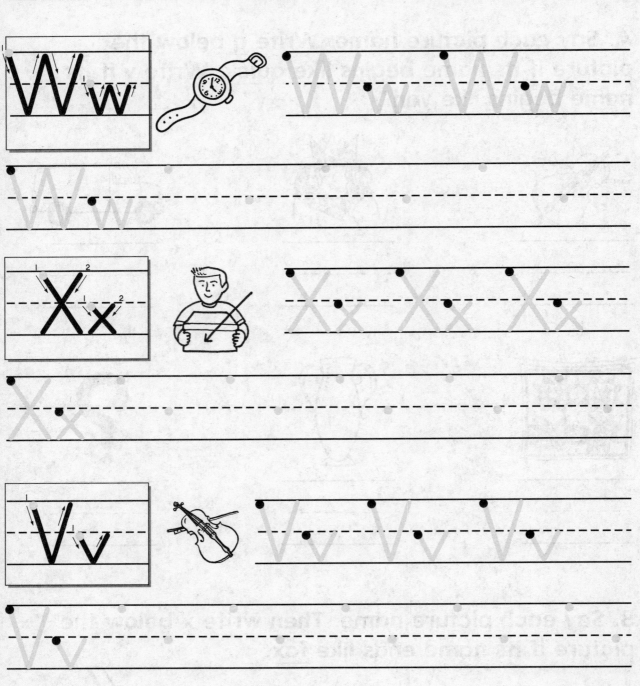

Write a sentence. Use the letters from this page.

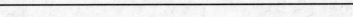

He and she go!

High-Frequency Words: and, have, said, see, was

④

He was ⌣.

He and She Go

①

See! He is ☺ _____.

③

"Have this," she said.

②

Name _____

A. Say each picture name. Write j below the picture if its name begins like jam. Write y if its name begins like yarn. Write z if its name begins like zoo.

B. Write j, y, or z to complete the words.

0

_____ ero _____ arn _____ am

Name _____

Name _____

The letter <u>a</u> can make the short **a** sound you hear in **h<u>a</u>t**.

Read the word. Listen for the short <u>a</u> sound. Circle the picture that the word names.

I. cat

2. fan

3. map

4. pan

Name _____

A. Complete each sentence.
Use one of the words in the box.

| does | not | school | what |

1. Sam can _____ see the map.

2. _____ do the cats have?

3. I like my _____ .

4. Where _____ Nan go?

B. Write your own sentence using a word from the box.

5. _____

_____

Name _____

Write a word from the box to name each picture.

bat	can	cat	fan	hat	pan

1. _____

2. _____

3. _____

4. _____

5. _____

6. _____

Name _____

Fill in the Key Details Chart. Use words from the story.

Detail
Detail
Detail

4

Jack likes to nap.

Jack is a cat.

Jack the Cat

1

Jack likes Tam.

③

Jack likes to play.

②

Name _____

A. Reread "Jack the Cat." Circle two pictures that show key details from the story.

1.

2.

3.

B. Draw a picture in the box that shows another key detail from the story.

Name _____

> Add **-s** to an action word when it follows a name or the word **he, she,** or **it.**
>
> I tag you.   He tags_ me.   Pam tags_ you.

Circle the word that completes each sentence.
Then write the word on the line.

1. She _____.
   nap   naps

2. He _____.
   bat   bats

3. It _____.
   quack   quacks

4. Max _____ for school.
   pack   packs

Name _____

> **Photographs** are pictures that show people, animals, and things in real life.

A. Look at the photograph. Use the photograph to complete the sentences.

©Ingram Publishing/SuperStock

_____

1. The cat has _____.

_____

2. The cat likes to _____

B. Look at the photograph. Write one more thing you see in the photograph.

_____

3. _____

Name _____

A. Read the draft model. Use the questions to help you focus on a single event.

> ### Draft Model
>
> We painted in class. I painted my family. I ate popcorn.

1. What event is the writing about?

2. What are the details in the writing?

3. What detail is not about the same event?

B. Now revise the draft to make sure all the details are about one event.

_____

- -

_____

_____

- -

_____

_____

- -

_____

Name _____

> The letter **i** can make the short **i** sound
> you hear in **p**i**n**.

Read the word. Listen for the short i sound. Circle the picture that the word names.

I. fin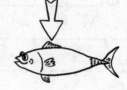

2. lid

3. hill

4. pig

Name _____

A. Complete each sentence. Use one of the words in the box.

down   out   up   very

1. The bag is _____ big.

2. Look _____ at my cat.

3. I go _____ to play.

4. Sam sits _____ .

B. Write your own sentence using a word from the box.

5. _____

_____

_____

Name _____

Write a word from the box to name each picture.

kiss	pin	pick	dig	win

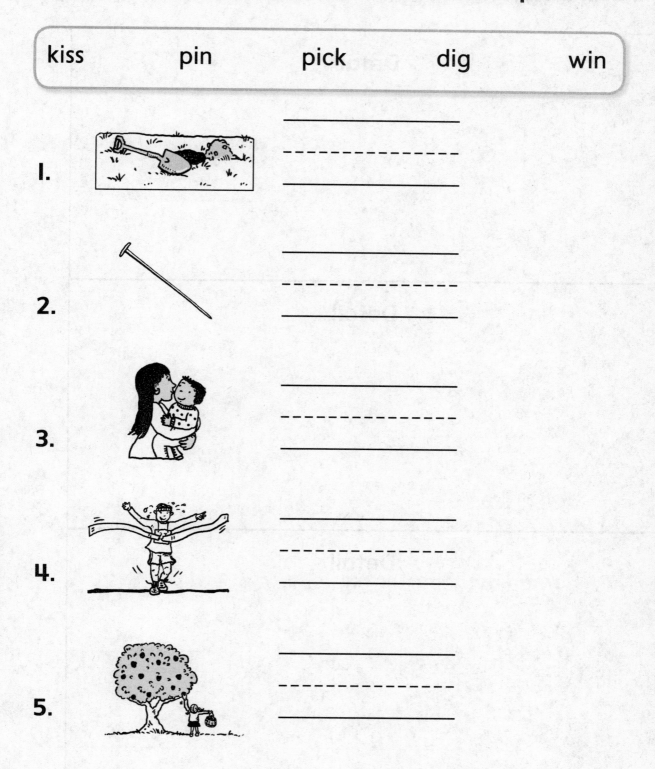

1. _____

2. _____

3. _____

4. _____

5. _____

Name _____

Fill in the Key Details Chart. Use words from the story.

Detail

Detail

Detail

Pip and Tip

Pip will go up.

Tip will sit.

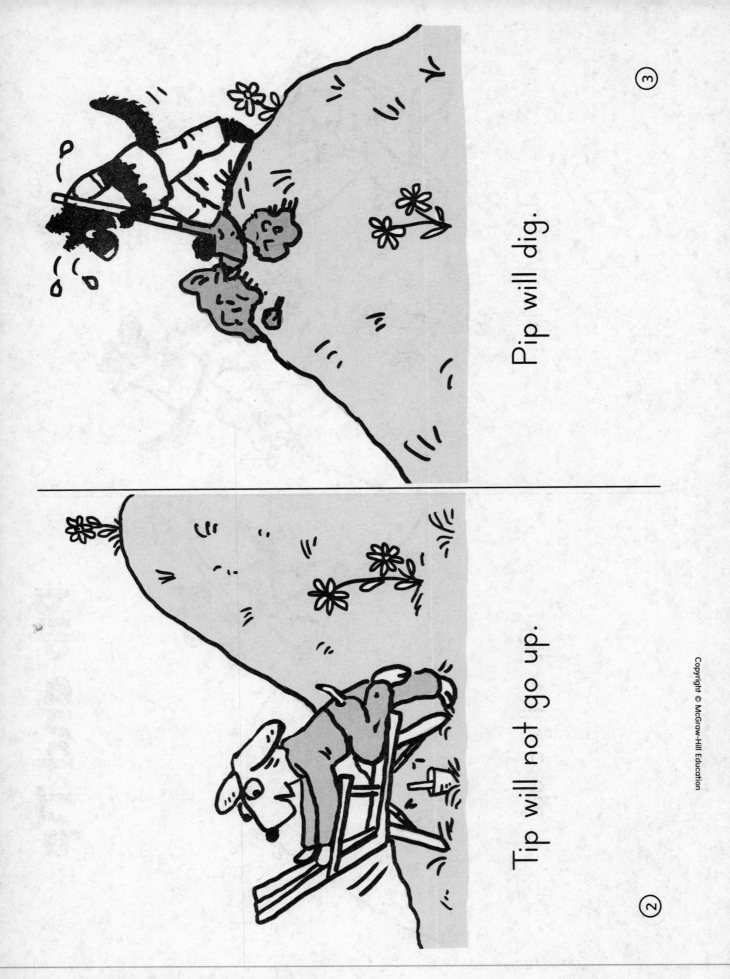

Pip will dig.

Tip will not go up.

③

②

Name _____

A. Reread "Pip and Tip." Circle two pictures that show key details from the story.

B. Write a sentence that tells a key detail from page 3.

_____

- -

_____

Name _____

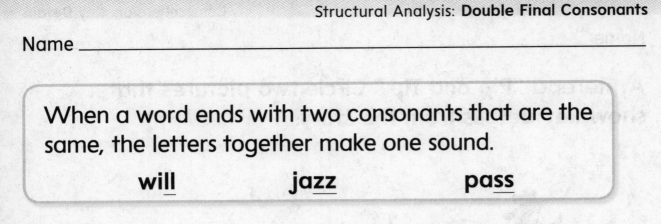

When a word ends with two consonants that are the same, the letters together make one sound.

will　　　　　**jazz**　　　　　**pass**

Read each sentence. Underline the word that ends with the same two consonants. Write the word on the line.

1. Matt has a big hat.

    _____
    - - - - - - - - - - - - - - - -
    _____

2. Pam has to miss school.

    _____
    - - - - - - - - - - - - - - - -
    _____

3. Cam will hit.

    _____
    - - - - - - - - - - - - - - - -
    _____

4. Dan can pass.

    _____
    - - - - - - - - - - - - - - - -
    _____

Name _____

> Authors use **bold print** to point out words that are important.

A. Look at the picture. Read the sentences. Underline the words in bold print.

1. The **city** is big.

2. It has lots of **buildings**.

3. This house is in the **country**.

4. Kids play in the big **yard**.

B. Write your own sentence about where you live. Circle the most important word.

5. _____
   _
   _____
   _
   _____

Name _____

A. Read the draft model. Use the questions to help you add describing details.

> ### Draft Model
>
> I share a room with my sister. We have bunk beds.
> My bed is on top.

1. What place is the writing about?

2. What are the describing details?

3. What other describing details could you add to the writing?

B. Now revise the draft by adding describing details to help readers picture the room in their minds.

_____

_____

_____

_____

Name _____

Sometimes consonants form a **blend**. You can hear the sound of a consonant and letter **l** form a blend at the beginning of **glad** and **slim**.

Read the word. Draw a line under the letters that form a blend. Write the letters. Circle the picture.

1. flag

2. clip

3. slip

4. clam

Name _____

A. Complete each sentence. Use one of the words in the box.

be	come	good	pull

1. Tam is a _____ cat.

2. Max can _____ the big pig.

3. I can _____ a big help.

4. Tip can _____ to me.

B. Write your own sentence using a word from the box.

5. _____

_____

_____

Name _____

Use a word from the box to complete each sentence.

| clap | flag | slam | black | glad |

1. We are _____.

2. The cat is _____.

3. Matt and Kim _____.

4. Do not _____ the door!

5. I can see a _____.

Name _____

Fill in the Key Details Chart. Use words from the story.

Detail

Detail

Detail

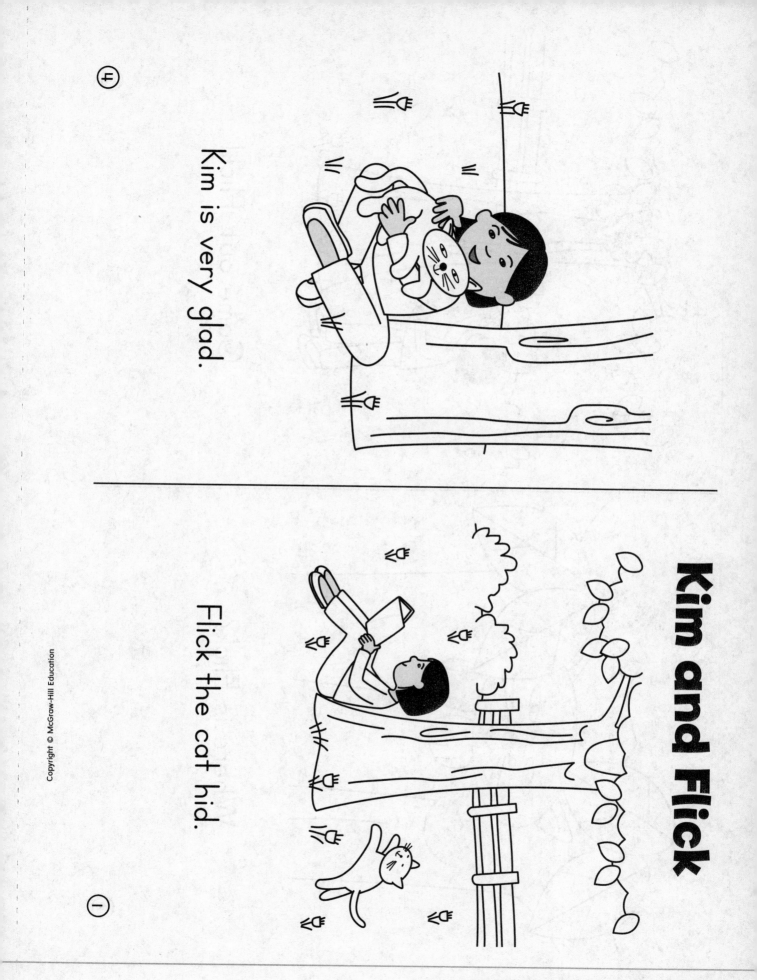

④

Kim is very glad.

Flick the cat hid.

Kim and Flick

①

Come out, Flick!

③

Where is Flick?

②

Name _____

A. Reread "Kim and Flick." Write a key detail to complete each sentence. Use a word from the box.

hid	Flick	come	Kim

1. _____ is a cat.

2. Flick _____ in the tree.

3. _____ looks for Flick.

4. Kim wants Flick to _____ out.

B. Draw a picture to show how Kim feels when she finds Flick.

Name _____

Some words end with **s̲**. When a word ends in one **s̲**, it means there is more than one of something.

flag 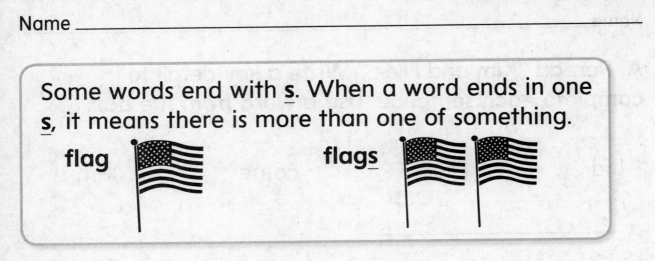 **flags̲**

Read each sentence. Underline the word that tells about more than one thing. Write the word on the line.

1. See the hats?

_____

- - - - - - - - - - - - - - - - - - -

_____

2. Tim and Jim have six bats.

_____

- - - - - - - - - - - - - - - - - - -

_____

3. We have cats.

_____

- - - - - - - - - - - - - - - - - - -

_____

4. The fish has fins.

_____

- - - - - - - - - - - - - - - - - - -

_____

Name _____

> **Labels** are words or phrases that name people or things shown in a picture or photograph.

Look at the pictures. Read the labels. Then use the labels to complete the sentences.

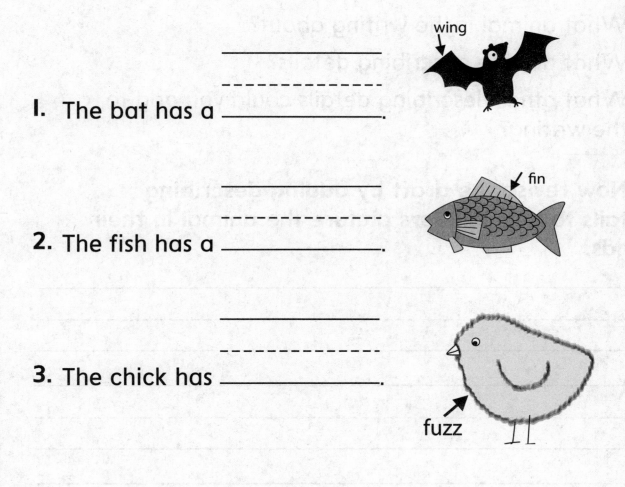

1. The bat has a _____.

2. The fish has a _____.

3. The chick has _____.

Name _____

A. Read the draft model. Use the questions to help you add describing details.

> ### Draft Model
> Tim is the class pet. Tim is a fish. Tim swims fast.

1. What animal is the writing about?

2. What are the describing details?

3. What other describing details could you add to the writing?

B. Now revise the draft by adding describing details to help readers picture the animal in their minds.

Name _____

> The letter **o** can make the short **o** sound
> you hear in **sock** and **dot**.

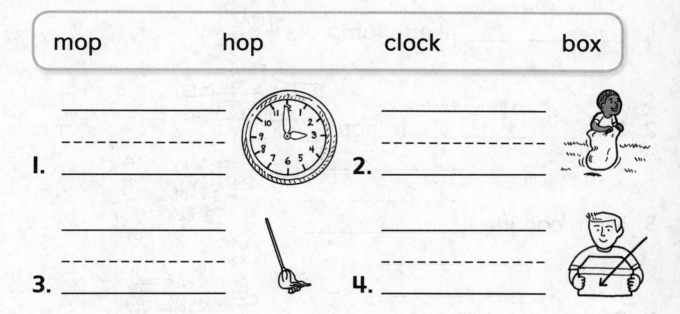

A. Read the words in the box. Listen for the short o sound. Write the word that names each picture.

mop	hop	clock	box

1. _____

2. _____

3. _____

4. _____

B. Circle each word that has the short o sound. Then write the word.

5. can   mom   clip   _____

6. fin   mat   top   _____

Name _____

A. Complete each sentence. Use one of the words in the box.

fun	make	they	too

_____

- - - - - - - - - - - - -

1. _____ like to jump.

_____

- - - - - - - - - - - - -

2. It is _____ to hop.

_____

- - - - - - - - - - - - -

3. Mom can jog, _____.

_____

- - - - - - - - - - - - -

4. Dad can _____ a cake.

B. Write your own sentence using a word from the box.

_____

- -

5. _____

_____

- -

_____

Name _____

Write a word from the box to name each picture.

ox	block	log	lock	mop	mom

1. _____

2. _____

3. _____

4. _____

5. _____

6. _____

Name _____

Fill in the Key Details Chart. Use words from the story.

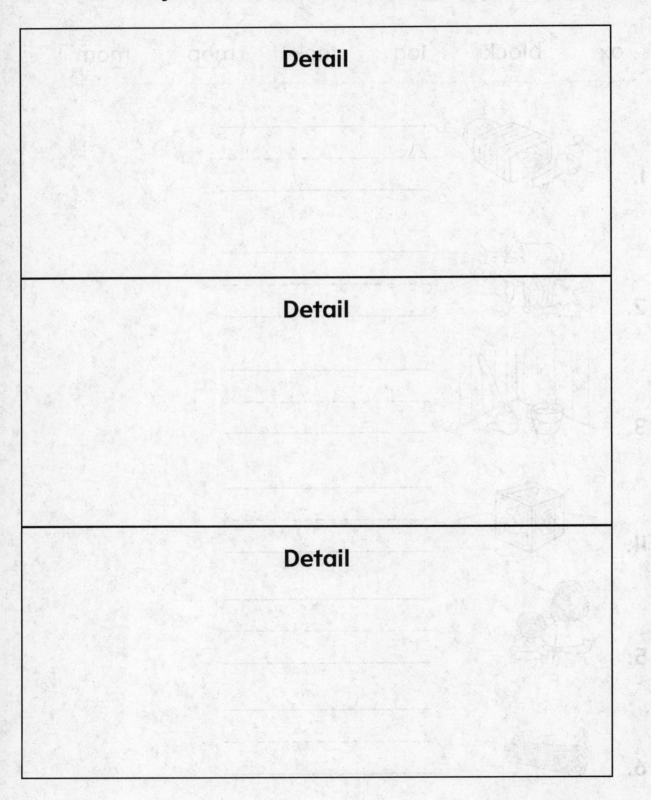

Detail

Detail

Detail

What Can It Do?

A dog can jog.

A cat can hop.

④

①

An ox can pull.

③

A fox can nap.

②

Name _____

Reread "What Can It Do?" Look for key details. Circle the word that answers each question.

1. What can a cat do?

   pull   hop

2. What can a dog do?

   jog   nap

3. Who can nap?

   a fox   an ox

4. Who can pull?

   an ox   a cat

Name _____

The letters of the alphabet always stay in the same order.

a b c d e f g h i j k l m n o p q r s t u v w x y z

Read the words in the box. Underline the first letter of each word. Write the words in ABC order. Use the pictures to help you.

ant	glass	sit	zip	jam

1. _____

2. _____

3. _____

4. _____

5. _____

Name _____

> Words in a poem can **rhyme**. Rhyming words have the same ending sound.
>
> m**op**   fl**op**   t**op**   p**op**

A. Read the poem. Circle the words that rhyme. Write the rhyming words on the lines.

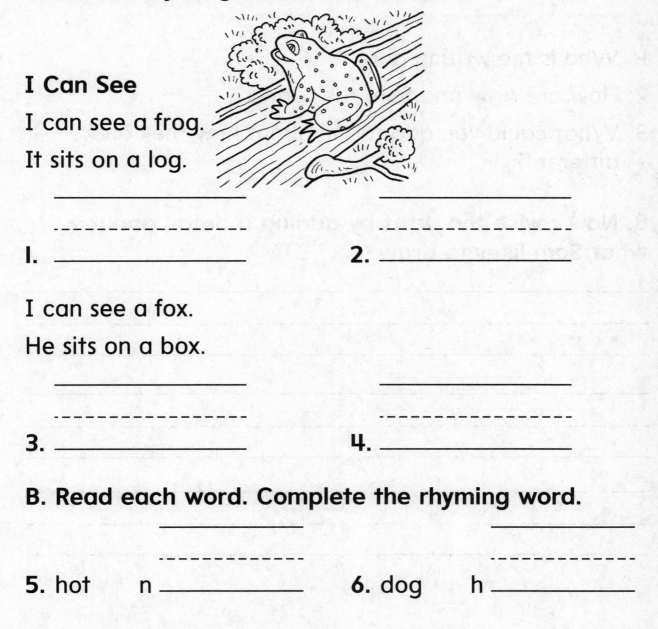

I Can See

I can see a frog.

It sits on a log.

1. _____   2. _____

I can see a fox.

He sits on a box.

3. _____   4. _____

B. Read each word. Complete the rhyming word.

5. hot   n _____   6. dog   h _____

Name _____

A. Read the draft model. Use the questions to help you write about how Sam and Amy are different.

> ### Draft Model
>
> Sam likes to draw. Amy likes to draw, too. Amy likes to draw dogs.

1. Who is the writing about?

2. How are Amy and Sam the same?

3. What could you add to tell about how they are different?

B. Now revise the draft by adding a detail about what Sam likes to draw.

_____

_____

_____

_____

_____

Name _____

Some words begin with a **consonant blend**. Listen to the beginning sounds in the word <u>crab</u>. You can hear the sound of each letter in the blend.

Read the word. Write the word. Circle the picture that it names.

1. frog

   _____
   - - - - - - - - - - - - - - - -
   _____

2. grass

   _____
   - - - - - - - - - - - - - - - -
   _____

3. crib

   _____
   - - - - - - - - - - - - - - - -
   _____

4. snap

   _____
   - - - - - - - - - - - - - - - -
   _____

Name _____

Write the word from the box that completes each sentence.

| jump | move | run | two |

1. I can _____

   I can _____.

2. I _____ a big box.

3. I can _____.

4. I have _____ cats.

Name _____

Read each word that begins with a consonant blend. Write the word from the box that names each picture.

| spill | crib | grass | drip | spin |

1. _____

2. _____

3. _____

4. _____

5. _____

Name _____

Fill in the Key Details Chart. Use details from the story.

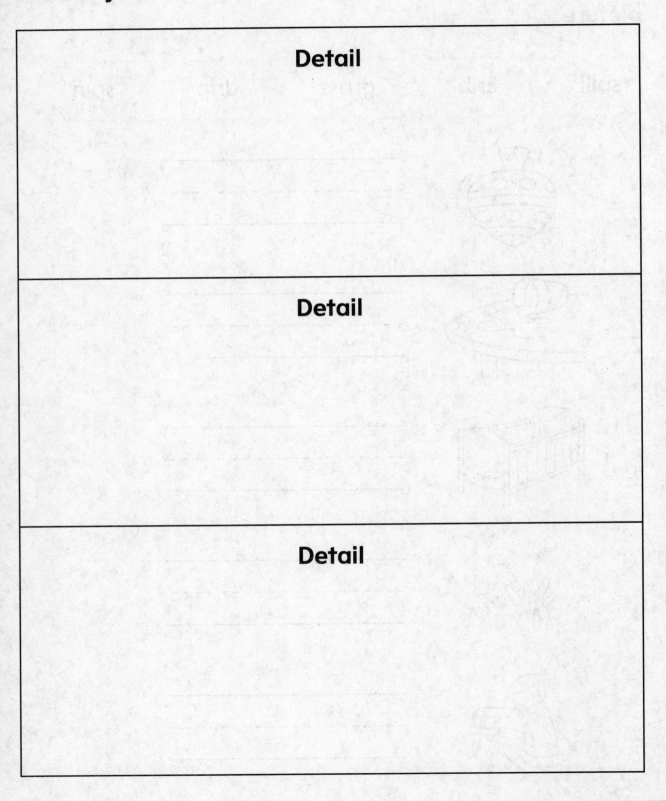

Detail
Detail
Detail

We are kids.
We can move.
We can have fun!

Kids Can Move

He can hop.

They can jump off.

③

She can run fast.

②

Name _____

Reread "Kids Can Move." Answer the questions.

1. Who can hop? Circle the picture.

2. Who runs fast? Draw a box around the picture.

3. How can kids move? Write two ways.

_____

- -

_____

4. Write two things kids can do.

_____   _____

- - - - - - - - - -   - - - - - - - - - -

_____   _____

Name _____

An **'s** at the end of a naming word means that something belongs to that person or thing.

Matt's hat

A. Underline the word that tells that something belongs to a person or thing. Write the word.

1. Dan's cat is little. _____

2. Pam's pals play. _____

3. This is my cat's mat. _____

B. Write a sentence to tell about something that belongs to someone you know. Use a word with 's.

4. _____

Name _____

A **diagram** is a picture with labels. The labels name the parts of the picture.

Look at the diagram of a cat. Use the words from the box to write the labels.

| back | leg | ear | eye |

Parts of a Cat

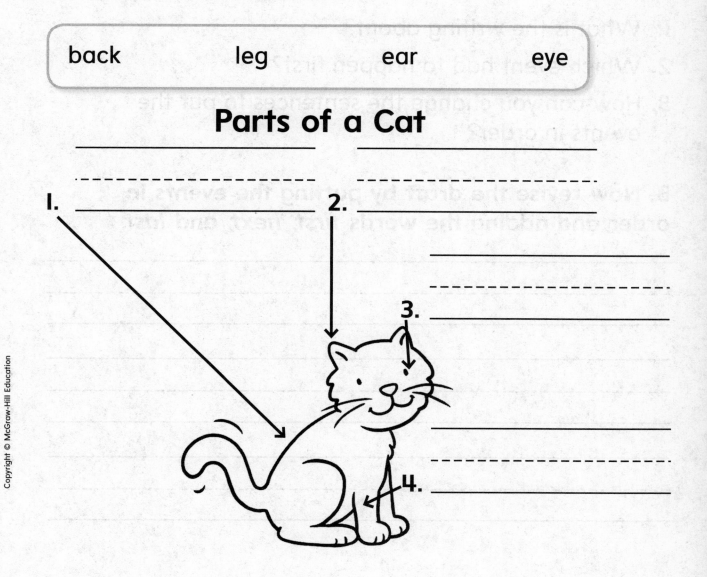

_____   _____

1. _____   2. _____

3. _____

4. _____

Name _____

A. Read the draft model. Use the questions to help you put the events in order.

> ### Draft Model
> I tied my shoes. I put my socks on. I put my shoes on.

1. What is the writing about?

2. Which event had to happen first?

3. How can you change the sentences to put the events in order?

B. Now revise the draft by putting the events in order and adding the words *first, next,* and *last.*

_____

- -

_____

- -

_____

- -

_____

- -

_____

Name _____

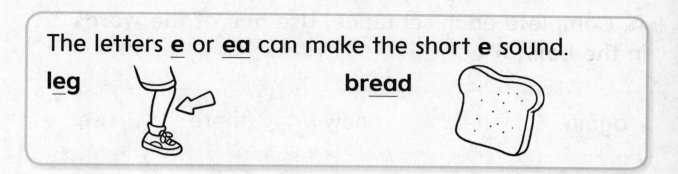

The letters **e** or **ea** can make the short **e** sound.

l__e__g   br__ea__d

A. Read the words in the box. Listen for the short e sound. Write the word that names each picture.

bed	vet	head	men

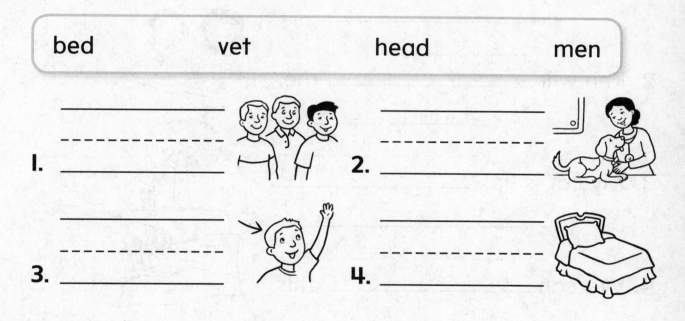

1. _____

2. _____

3. _____

4. _____

B. Write your own sentence using a word from the box.

5. _____

Name _____

A. Complete each sentence. Use one of the words in the box.

again	help	new	there	use

1. This hat is _____.

2. Ken will _____ me.

3. My cat is up _____.

4. We can _____ this.

5. Ned will try _____.

B. Write your own sentence using a word from the box.

6. _____

Name _____

Use a word in the box to complete each sentence.

| dress | bread | ten | pet | egg | head |

_____

1. This nest has an _____.

_____

2. Dan will have _____.

_____

3. Ben has _____ hats.

_____

4. Max is a good _____

_____

5. Nan has a new _____

_____

6. Pat has a hat on his _____.

Name _____

Fill in the Character, Setting, Events Chart. Use words from the story.

Character	Setting	Events

④

They fix the clock.
The man is glad!

A Fun Job

A clock can stop.
Mom can fix it!

①

A man comes in.
Can Mom and Ben
fix his clock?

③

Ben helps his mom.
Ben likes his job.

②

Name _____

A. Reread "A Fun Job."

Write <u>C</u> if the sentence and picture tell about a character.

Write <u>S</u> if the sentence and picture tell about a setting.

Write <u>E</u> if the sentence and picture tell about an event.

I. Ben likes his job.

_____

- - - - - - - - - - - - -

_____

2. The shop has clocks.

_____

- - - - - - - - - - - - -

_____

3. They fix the clock.

_____

- - - - - - - - - - - - -

_____

Name _____

Add the ending **-ed** to an action word to tell about something that already happened.

help   **help**_ed_

A. Add -ed to each word. Write the word on the line.

1. spill + ed   =   _____

2. smell + ed   =   _____

3. dress + ed   =   _____

4. mix + ed   =   _____

B. Use a word you wrote above to complete the sentence.

5. I _____ the bread.

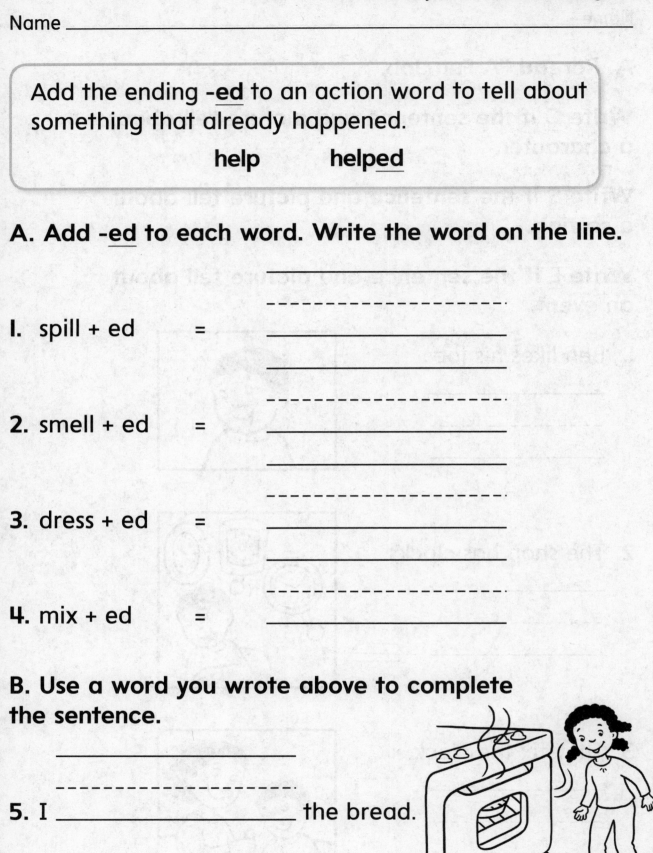

Name _____

A **label** is a word or phrase that names things in a picture or photograph.

Look at the fire truck. Use a word from the box to write each label.

ladder   light   hose

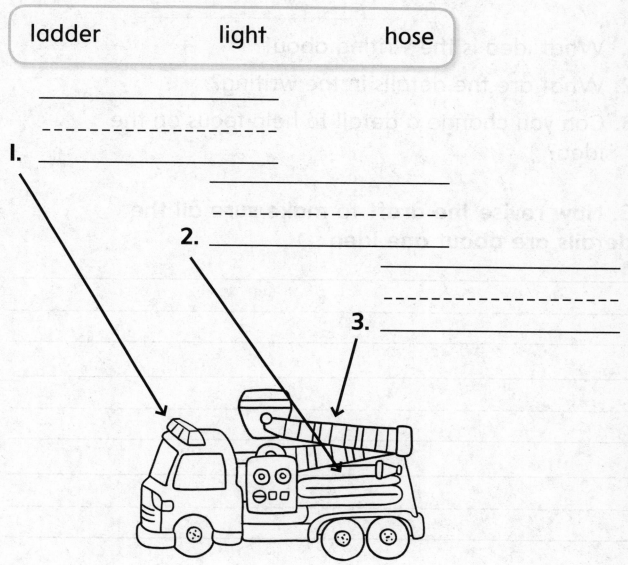

1. _____

2. _____

3. _____

Name _____

A. Read the draft model. Use the questions to help you focus on one idea.

> ### Draft Model
> Teachers work hard. They plan lessons. They have families.

1. What idea is the writing about?

2. What are the details in the writing?

3. Can you change a detail to help focus on the idea?

B. Now revise the draft to make sure all the details are about one idea.

_____

_____

_____

_____

_____

_____

Name _____

> The letter **u** can make the short **u** sound you hear in **rug**.

A. Read the words. Listen for the short u sound. Write the word that names each picture.

> cut   bug   hut   duck   pup

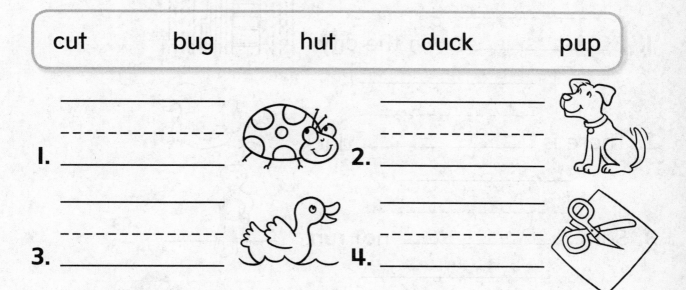

1. _____

2. _____

3. _____

4. _____

B. Write your own sentence using a word from the box.

5. _____

_____

Name _____

Complete each sentence. Use one of the words in the box.

three	could	live	one	then

_____
- - - - - - - - - - - - - -
1. I _____ in the city.

_____
- - - - - - - - - - - - - -
2. There is _____ duck.

_____
- - - - - - - - - - - - - -
3. Sam _____ not run.

_____
- - - - - - - - - - - - - -
4. She has _____ pups.

5. I run up the hill.

_____
- - - - - - - - - - - - - -
_____ I run down the hill.

Name _____

Write a word from the box to describe each picture.

| sun | bus | up | drum | mud |

1. _____
   - - - - - - - - - - - - - - -
   _____

2. _____
   - - - - - - - - - - - - - - -
   _____

3. _____
   - - - - - - - - - - - - - - -
   _____

4. _____
   - - - - - - - - - - - - - - -
   _____

5. _____
   - - - - - - - - - - - - - - -
   _____

Name _____

Fill in the Character, Setting, Events Chart. Use details from the story.

Character	Setting	Events

"Cub plays a jug.
The pals have fun!

Pals Play and Hum

Look at Bug.
Bug can hum.

Do you see Frog?
Frog can drum.

③

Look at Duck!
Duck can pluck.

②

Name _____

Reread "Pals Play and Hum."
Follow the directions.

1. Write a sentence that tells where Bug is on page 1.

_____

- -

_____

2. Write the word that tells what Duck can do.

_____

- - - - - - - - - - - - - - - - - - -

_____

3. Write the word that tells what Frog can do.

_____

- - - - - - - - - - - - - - - - - - -

_____

4. Write a sentence that tells what the pals do.

_____

- -

_____

Name _____

> A **contraction** is when you put two words together to make one word.
>
> **He's** is a shorter way of saying **he is**.
> The apostrophe (') stands for the missing letter **i** in **is**.

A. Read the two words. Write the contraction.

1. she is _____

2. it is _____

3. he is _____

4. let us _____

B. Write your own sentence using a contraction.

5. _____

Name _____

> **Captions** are short descriptions that tell more about a photograph or picture.

Circle the caption that tells about the picture.

1. Jon gets on the bus.
Jon is at school.

2. Here is a farm.
Here is a pet shop.

3. The park is big.
The house is big.

4. Dan has a new bike.
Dan has a new pal.

5. They get in a cab.
They get on bikes.

Name _____

A. Read the draft model. Use the questions to help you add a beginning sentence that names the topic.

Draft Model

There are rows of bookshelves. The bookshelves are filled. Some cool magazines are on top of the shelves.

---

1. What is the topic of the writing?

2. What details tell about the topic?

3. What information could you include in a beginning sentence?

B. Now revise the draft by adding a beginning sentence that names the topic.

_____

_____

_____

_____

_____

Name _____

Sometimes words end with a **blend** of sounds. You can hear each consonant sound in an **end blend**.

ne<u>st</u>   si<u>nk</u>

A. Read the words in the box. Listen for the end blend. Write the word that names each picture. Underline the end blend.

| list | hand | tent | bank | desk | lamp |

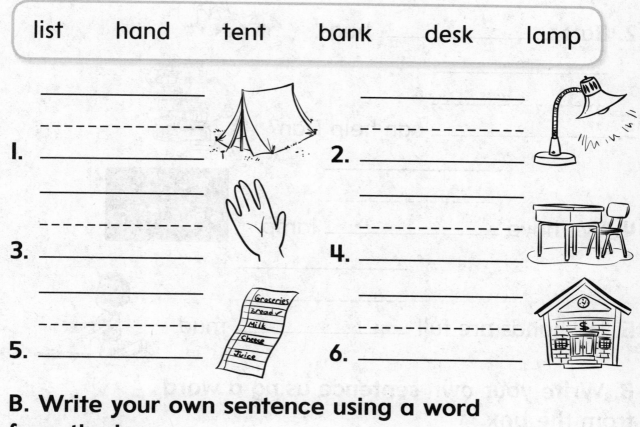

1. _____

2. _____

3. _____

4. _____

5. _____

6. _____

B. Write your own sentence using a word from the box.

7. _____

Name _____

A. Complete each sentence. Use one of the words in the box.

eat	no	of	under	who

_____

1. The cat is _____ the desk.

_____

2. Bats _____ bugs.

_____

3. _____ can help Dan?

_____

4. We have _____ lamp.

_____

5. His hands are full _____ mud.

B. Write your own sentence using a word from the box.

_____

6. _____

Name _____

Read each sentence. Underline a word that has an end blend. Write the word.

1. Bob will send a box to Jan. _____

2. Pam did the best job. _____

3. My dog likes to jump up. _____

4. Set the cup in the sink. _____

5. I will go ask Dad. _____

6. I see a bug on the plant. _____

Name _____

Fill in the Main Topic and Details Chart.
Use details from the story.

Main Topic		
Detail	**Detail**	**Detail**

④

Here are three bats.
Bats can spin!

This is Big Rock Pond.
What can we see?

Big Rock Pond

①

Here are two frogs.
Two frogs jump.

③

Here is one bug.
A bug can buzz and buzz.

②

Name _____

A. Reread "Big Rock Pond." Write the main topic to tell what it is about. Write the key details to tell more about the topic. Use the sentences from the box.

Bugs buzz.

Frogs jump.

Things live at the pond.

Bats spin.

Topic:

_____

_____

Key Detail: _____

_____

Key Detail: _____

_____

Key Detail: _____

Name _____

> Add the ending **-ing** to an action word to tell what is happening now.
>
> **jump**   **jumping**

A. Add **-ing** to each word. Write the new word.

1. ask + ing   =   _____

2. rest + ing   =   _____

3. pack + ing   =   _____

4. help + ing   =   _____

5. plant + ing   =   _____

B. Use a word you wrote above to complete the sentence.

6. She is _____ a bag.

Name _____

> Songs have a pattern and a beat. Poems can have a pattern and a beat, too. The same words can be used over and over. This is called **repetition**.
>
> A bug can buzz. Buzz, buzz, bug!

Read the pairs of sentences. Circle the sentences that have the same words used over and over.

1. The cat sits on a mat.
It will nap.

2. See me up in the tree.
I am up, up, up in the tree.

3. Fred hops a lot.
Hop, Fred, hop!

4. A fish is in the pond.
It has fins.

5. In the car, they go far.
Go, go, go in the car.

6. Nat hugs his bear.
Jan holds her kitten.

Name _____

A. Read the draft model. Use the questions to help you add facts to the writing.

> ### Draft Model
>
> Many kinds of fish live in the ocean. Fish can be big or small. Some fish like to swim together.

I. What is the topic of your writing?

2. What details tell about the main idea?

3. What facts could you add to the writing?

B. Now revise the draft by adding facts to the writing.

_____

- - - - - - - - - - - - - - - - - - - -

_____

- - - - - - - - - - - - - - - - - - - -

_____

- - - - - - - - - - - - - - - - - - - -

_____

Name _____

> The letters **sh** make the ending sound in **fish**.
>
> The letters **th** make the beginning sound in **thin**.
>
> The letters **ng** make the ending sound in **ring**.

Read each sentence. Circle the word that has sh, th, or ng. Write the word.

_____

1. Here is a fresh plum.

_____

2. Min and Dan like to sing.

_____

3. A bug can sting!

_____

4. Say thank you for a gift.

_____

5. Sam and Dad pick up shells.

_____

6. I like to play with my pals.

Name _____

Match each sentence to the picture.

1. I **want** that one.

a.

2. We **all** have a snack.

b.

3. What **day** is this?

c.

4. **Her** socks have dots.

d.

5. I use this to **call** Dad.

e.

Name _____

A. Circle the word that names each picture.

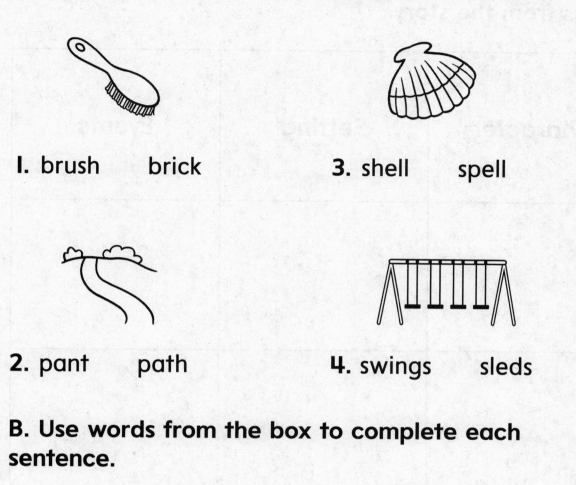

1. brush   brick

3. shell   spell

2. pant   path

4. swings   sleds

B. Use words from the box to complete each sentence.

math	fish	sting	think

5. A _____ can swim.

6. We have _____ in school.

Name _____

Fill in the Character, Setting, Events Chart. Use details from the story.

Character	Setting	Events

(4)

All the dogs help.
They see the play!

All Help with the Play

Let's have a play.
We can all help.

(1)

What can we do?
We want to help.

③

Rex makes fun hats.
Shep makes tops with dots.

②

Name _____

**Reread "All Help with the Play."
Circle the word that answers
each question. Write the word.**

1. The story characters are _____.

         dogs   hats

2. They will do a _____.

         game   play

3. Who makes fun hats? _____

         Shep   Rex

4. What do the other dogs do? _____

      See the play   make hats

Name _____

When a syllable ends in a consonant and has one vowel letter, the vowel sound is usually short. This is called a **closed syllable.**

rab/bit   bas/ket   cab/in

Read each word. Draw a line between the syllables. Write each syllable on a line.

1. napkin   _____   _____

2. locket   _____   _____

3. finish   _____   _____

4. pumpkin   _____   _____

5. magnet   _____   _____

Name _____

> A **list** organizes things and ideas.

A. Read the words in the box. Place each word in the list where it belongs.

> eggs   sing   ham   read   swim   jam

Things to Eat

_____

_____

_____

_____

_____

Things to Do

_____

_____

_____

_____

_____

B. Add one more thing to each list.

Things to Eat

_____

_____

Things to Do

_____

_____

Name _____

A. Read the draft model. Use the questions to help you add a beginning and a middle to the story.

> **Draft Model**
>
> Pat's house is clean now. The floor is shiny. The trash is gone.

1. What is the story about?

2. What details tell about the end of the story?

3. What could you add to the beginning and the middle of the story?

B. Now revise the draft by adding a beginning and a middle to the story.

_____

— — — — — — — — — — — — — — — — — — — —

_____

— — — — — — — — — — — — — — — — — — — —

_____

— — — — — — — — — — — — — — — — — — — —

_____

Name _____

> The letters **ch** and **tch** stand for the sound you hear at the beginning of **chip** and the end of **ditch**. The letters **wh** stand for the sound at the beginning of **when**. The letters **ph** stand for the sound at the end of **graph**.

Read the words in the box. Match each word with a sound-spelling below. Write the word.

whisk	chin	Phil	graph
pitch	lunch	when	catch

1. wh _____ _____

2. ch _____ _____

3. ph _____ _____

4. tch _____ _____

Name _____

A. Complete each sentence. Use one of the words in the box.

walk	many	by	place	around

1. Ned sits _____ the tree.

2. She has _____ socks.

3. This is a good _____ to eat.

4. Ed will _____ fast.

5. We go _____ the rock.

B. Write your own sentence using a word from the box.

6. _____

Name _____

A. Use <u>ch</u> or <u>tch</u> to complete the word that names the picture.

1. _____ i n

2. c r u _____

3. h a _____

4. l u n _____

B. Write <u>wh</u> to complete each word.

5. _____ e n

6. _____ i c h

C. Write <u>ph</u> to complete the word.

7. g r a _____

D. Write a sentence using a word from above.

8. _____

_____

_____

Name _____

Fill in the Main Topic and Key Details Chart.
Use details from the story.

Main Topic		
Detail	**Detail**	**Detail**

④

Look around this place.
Many dogs fetch.

①

Look Around

Look around this place.
Some chicks hatch.

Look around this place.
Lots of buses whiz by.

③

Look around this place.
Many kids play catch.

②

Name _____

Read the story and follow the directions.

1. Write the word that tells you what chicks do.

_____

- -

_____

2. Write the word that tells what kids play.

_____

- -

_____

3. Write what buses do.

_____

- -

_____

4. Write the main topic of "Look Around."

_____

- -

_____

Name _____

Add the ending -**es** to naming words that end in **ss**, **z**, **x**, **sh**, and **ch** to make them mean "more than one."

dish + es = dish**es**

A. Add -**es** to make the word mean "more than one."

_____

- -

I. peach _____

_____

- -

2. box _____

_____

- -

3. dress _____

_____

- -

4. brush _____

B. Circle the word that means "more than one."

5. glass   glasses   6. foxes   fox

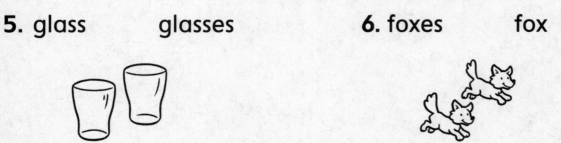

Name _____

> A **map** shows where places are found. North, south, east, and west are **directions.** They are shown on a compass. Use directions to tell where things are.

Look at the map. Circle the answer to each question.

1. Is the slide north or south of the swings?

   north   south

2. What is west of the slide?

   bench   see-saw

3. What is north of the bench?

   gate   tree

Name _____

A. Read the draft model. Use the questions to help you add supporting details.

> ### Draft Model
>
> Open the door and walk inside. Turn down the hallway. There is the lunchroom.

1. What are the directions about?

2. How do the directions help you find your way?

3. What supporting details could you add to the directions?

B. Now revise the draft by adding supporting details to the directions.

_____

_____

_____

_____

_____

_____

Name _____

> The word **at** has a short **a** sound.
>
> Add **e** to the end to make **ate**.
>
> The **a_e** spelling makes the long **a** sound in **ate**.

A. Read the words in the box. Listen for the long a sound. Write the word that names each picture.

> gate   tape   snake   grape

1. _____

2. _____

3. _____

4. _____

B. Write your own sentence using a word from the box.

5. _____

_____

_____

Name _____

Match each sentence to the picture.

1. I can not go out **today**.

a.

2. He can have **some** grapes.

b.

3. This is the **way** to camp.

c.

4. I see the school **now**.

d.

5. **Why** is the pup sad?

e.

6. I can put this **away**.

f.

Name _____

Use the words in the box to complete the sentences.

| late | shape | lake | chase | whale | tape |

1. A _____ can swim.

2. Tam can use _____ on the box.

3. Ken is _____ for school.

4. What _____ is this?

5. I see hills by the _____.

6. Jen will _____ me.

Name _____

Fill in the Sequence Chart. Use words from the story.

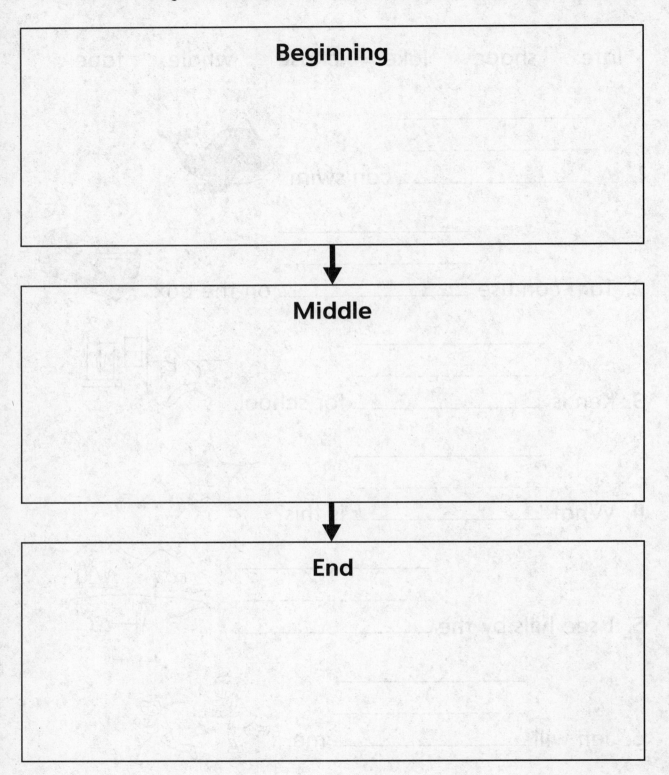

Beginning

↓

Middle

↓

End

Now, Whale is in.
The pals have fun!

Whale is on skates.
He is going to the lake.

Whale at the Lake

①

"Here we are!" they yell.
They wave to Whale and
tell him to come in.

③

Whale can't see his pals.
Where did they go?

②

Name _____

A. Reread "Whale at the Lake."

Write <u>I</u> if the sentence and picture tell what happened at the beginning.

Write <u>2</u> if the sentence and picture tell something that happened in the middle.

Write <u>3</u> if the sentence and picture tell what happened at the end.

I. Whale plays with his pals.

_____

- - - - - - - - - - - - - -

_____

2. Whale sees his pals.

_____

- - - - - - - - - - - - - -

_____

3. Whale skates to the lake.

_____

- - - - - - - - - - - - - -

_____

Name _____

> A **contraction** is a short form of two words. An
> **apostrophe** (') takes the place of the missing letters.
>
> **is + not = isn't**
>
> The apostrophe (') in **isn't** stands for the letter <u>o</u>.

A. Write the contraction for the two words.

_____

- .

1. has + not = _____.

_____

- .

2. are + not = _____.

_____

- .

3. was + not = _____.

_____

- .

4. can + not = _____.

B. Use a contraction you wrote above to complete the sentence.

_____

- - - - - - - - - - - - - - - - - -

5. Nate _____ go!

Name _____

> A word that is in **bold print** is an important word.

A. Read the sentences. Circle the words in bold print.

I. A **watch** can help you tell time.

2. This **clock** can ring to get you up.

3. A **calendar** tells you what day it is.

B. Use the words in bold print to help you answer the question.

4. What tells you the day?

_____

- -

_____

Name _____

A. Read the draft model. Use the questions to help you add details with sensory words.

> **Draft Model**
>
> The bell rings and we go to lunch. I sit and eat my sandwich first. I eat an apple next.

I. What is the topic of the writing?

2. What details tell about the topic?

3. What sensory words could you add to tell more details about the topic?

B. Now revise the draft by adding sensory words to tell how the bell sounds and how the foods look, feel, and taste.

_____

_____

_____

_____

_____

_____

Name _____

> The word **rid** has a short **i** sound.
>
> Add **e** to the end to make **ride**.
>
> The **i_e** spelling makes the long **i** sound you hear in **ride**.

A. Read the words in the box. Listen for the long i sound. Write the word that names each picture.

smile	dime	kite	bike

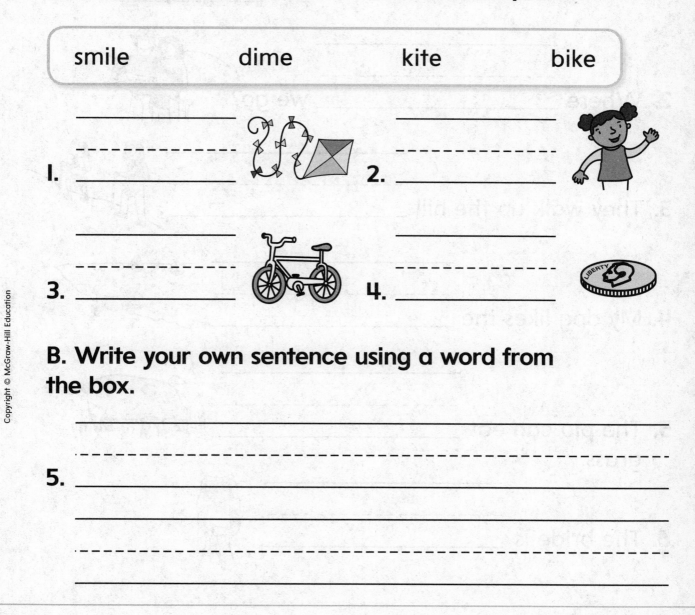

1. _____

2. _____

3. _____

4. _____

B. Write your own sentence using a word from the box.

5. _____

_____

Name _____

Complete each sentence. Use one of the words in the box.

| green | grow | together | should | pretty | water |

1. He will _____ tall.

2. Where _____ we go?

3. They walk up the hill _____.

4. My dog likes the _____.

5. The pig can eat _____ grass.

6. The bride is _____.

Name _____

Read the words. Circle the word that has the long i sound. Write the word on the line.

1. fin   pin   fine   _____

2. nine   his   nip   _____

3. will   slide   slid   _____

4. bit   lick   bite   _____

5. pine   pin   dip   _____

6. mill   in   mine   _____

Name _____

Fill in the Sequence Chart. Use words from the story.

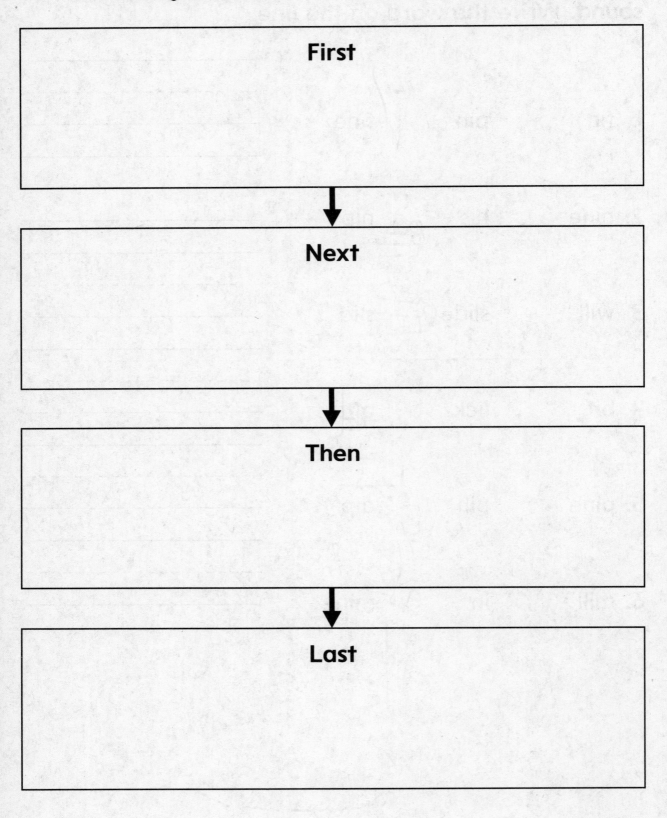

First

Next

Then

Last

④

Mom: I love plants.
You made me smile!
Kate: We are glad!
Mike: Get well, Mom!

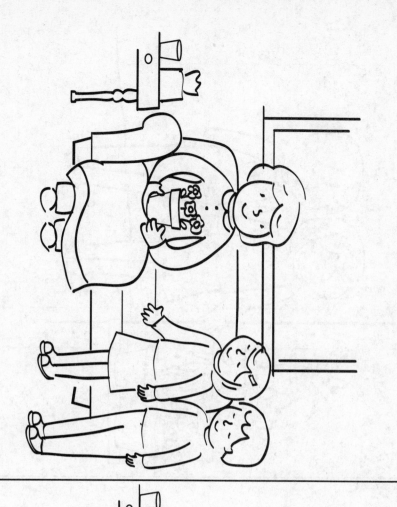

A Gift for Mom

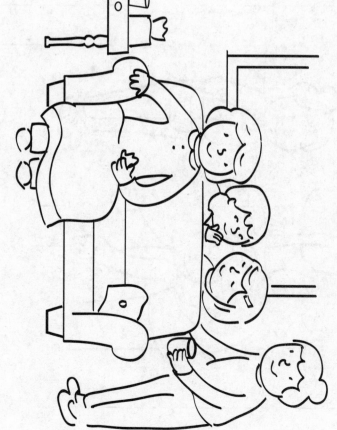

Mike: Mom is sick.
Kate: Let's get a gift.

①

Mike: Look! Plants!
Kate: Mom likes plants.

③

Mike: I can shop.
Kate: Let's go together.

②

Name _____

Reread "A Gift for Mom." Follow the directions.

1. Write a sentence that tells what happens first in the story.

   _____

   -

   _____

2. Write a sentence that tells you what Kate wants to do.

   _____

   -

   _____

3. Write a sentence that tells what happens next.

   _____

   -

   _____

4. How does Mom feel at the end of the story?

   _____

   -

   _____

Name _____

You can add **-s** to the end of a word to name more than one person or thing.

bike 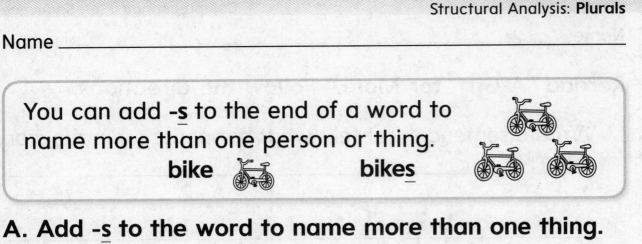 **bikes**

A. Add -s to the word to name more than one thing. Write the new word.

1. kite _____ S _____

2. pile _____ S _____

3. grape _____

4. dime _____ 2 _____

5. snake _____ S _____

B. Write your own sentence. Use a word that names more than one thing.

6. 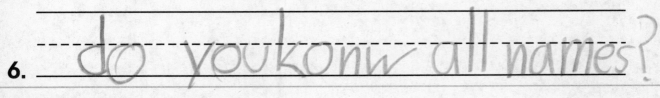 do youkonw all names?

Name _____

> **Diagrams** are pictures that have labels. The labels tell about the parts.

Look at the diagram of a plant. Use the words from the box to complete the diagram.

| flower | leaf | root | stem |

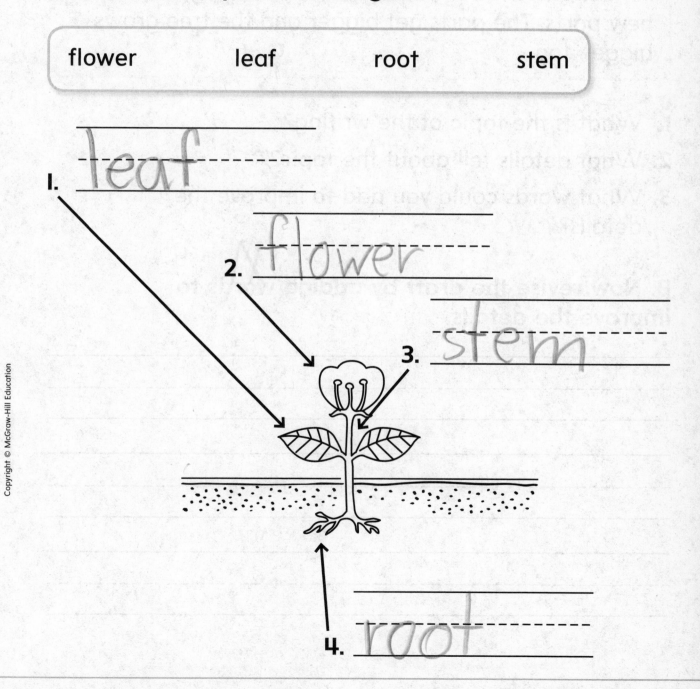

1. leaf

2. flower

3. stem

4. root

Name _____

A. Read the draft model. Use the questions to help you add words to create a clear picture of the tree.

> ## Draft Model
>
> At first a new tree is small. Then the tree grows new parts. The parts get bigger and the tree grows bigger, too.

1. What is the topic of the writing?

2. What details tell about the topic?

3. What words could you add to improve the details?

B. Now revise the draft by adding words to improve the details.

_____

_____

_____

_____

_____

_____

Name _____

Sometimes the letter **c** makes the **s** sound. You can hear it in **race** and **nice**.

The letter **g** can make the **j** sound. You hear it in **wage** and **gel**.

The letters **dge** together also make the **j** sound, as in **badge** and **ledge**.

Say the word. Write the word. Circle the picture that shows the word.

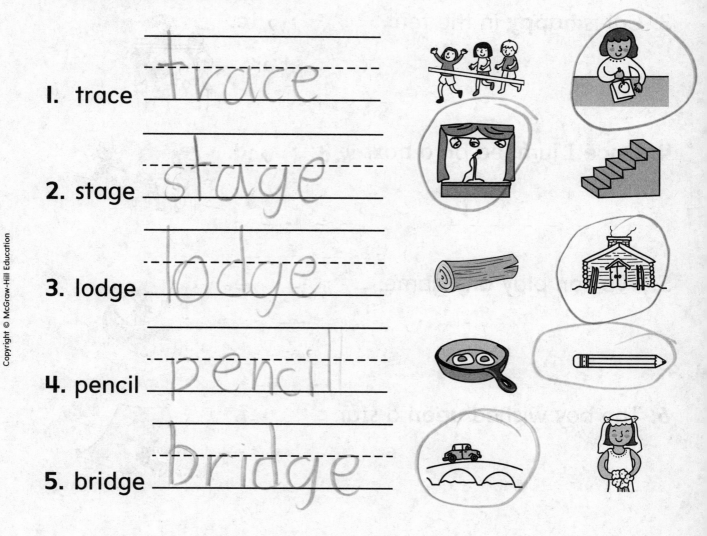

1. trace _trace_

2. stage _stage_

3. lodge _lodge_

4. pencil _pencil_

5. bridge _bridge_

Name _____

Match each sentence to the picture.

1. I was **so** fast, I won the race.

a.

2. The fish came **from** the pond.

b.

3. Cal is **happy** in the tent.

c.

4. **Once** I jumped on a box.

d.

5. We can play **any** game.

e.

6. The boy wished **upon** a star.

f.

Name _____

Use the words in the box to complete the sentences.

| hedge | dance | nice | cage | edge |

1. Pip sits in a __cage__ .

2. Mom cuts the top __edge__ of the can.

3. Ed trims the __hedge__ .

4. Pam is __nice__ .

5. Ann likes to __dance__ .

Name _____

Fill in the Cause and Effect Chart. Use words from the story.

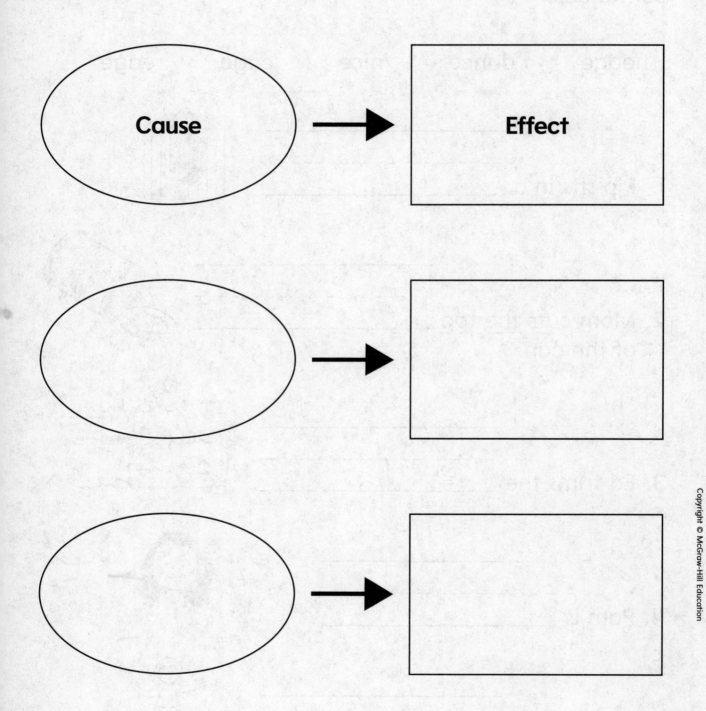

Cause ➤ Effect

④

Little Buck helped Fred.
They got to Gran's.
They had fudge!

Little Fred and Little Buck

Gran liked fudge.
Mom was making some.
Fred walked to Gran's with it.

①

Little Buck came by.
"Can you help me?"
asked Fred.

③

There are too many trees.
Where is the path? Little
Fred is lost!

②

Name _____

Reread "Little Fred and Little Buck." Answer the questions.

1. What causes Little Fred to go to Gran's?

gran like's fudge

2. What causes Fred to get lost?

There war too many trees

3. What is the effect of meeting Little Buck?

little buck came by

4. What is the effect of going to Gran's?

she like's fudge

Name _____

> Add -**ed** to an action word to tell what happened in the past. Add -**ing** to an action word to tell what is happening now.
>
> Look at the word **race**. It ends with the letter **e**. To add -**ed** or -**ing**, first drop the **e**.
>
> ra**ce** – e + **ed** = ra**ced**
> ra**ce** – e + **ing** = ra**cing**

A. Add -**ed** to each word. Write the new word.

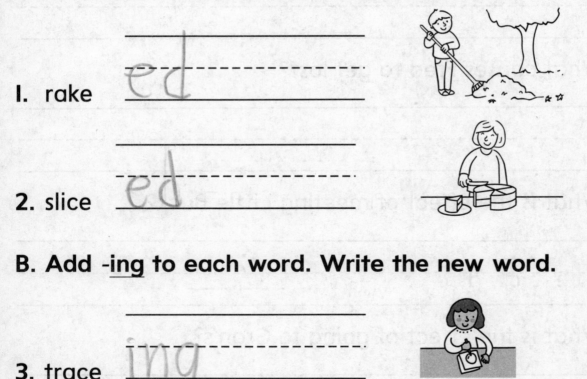

I. rake _____ed_____

2. slice _____ed_____

B. Add -**ing** to each word. Write the new word.

3. trace _____ing_____

4. skate _____ing_____

Name _____

Words in a song or poem sometimes **rhyme**.
Words that rhyme have the same ending sound.
Say the words in each column to hear the rhyme.

cl<u>ap</u>	b<u>est</u>	b<u>ell</u>
sl<u>ap</u>	r<u>est</u>	w<u>ell</u>
fl<u>ap</u>	n<u>est</u>	f<u>ell</u>

Say the words. Cross out the word that does not rhyme. Write a new rhyming word.

I. <u>ate</u>, <u>plate</u>, ~~that~~, <u>date</u>   skate   *skate*

2. fine, nine, dine, ~~pin~~   mine

3. <u>mice</u>, ~~pick~~, <u>dice</u>, <u>ice</u>   rice   *rice*
   slice

4. ~~has~~, cr<u>ash</u>, sm<u>ash</u>, d<u>ash</u>   mash

Name _____

A. Read the draft model. Use the questions to help you add strong verbs to the writing.

> ### Draft Model
>
> The little girl ran fast to get the cat. Then the cat got scared and ran fast. The cat got away.

1. What is the topic of the story?

2. What verbs are in the story?

3. What strong verbs could you add to the story to make it more exciting?

B. Now revise the draft by adding strong verbs to make it more exciting.

_____

_____

_____

_____

_____

_____

Name _____

The letters **o_e** stand for the long **o** sound.
The long **o** sound is the middle sound in **rope**.

The letters **u_e** stand for the long **u** sound.
The long **u** sound is the first sound in **use**.

The letters **e_e** stand for the long **e** sound.
The long **e** sound is the middle sound in **Pete**.

A. Look at each picture. Circle the word that names the picture. Write the word.

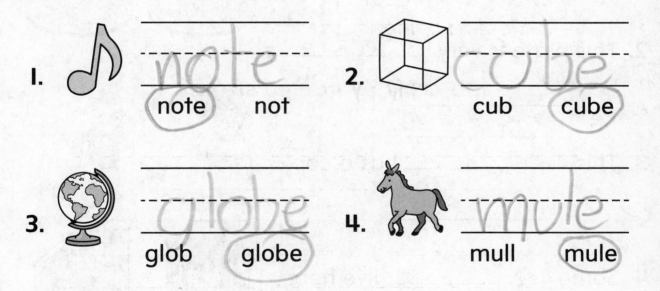

1. ~~note~~   (note)   not

2. ~~cube~~   cub   (cube)

3. ~~globe~~   glob   (globe)

4. ~~mule~~   mull   (mule)

B. Look at each picture. Write o, u, or e to complete the word that names it.

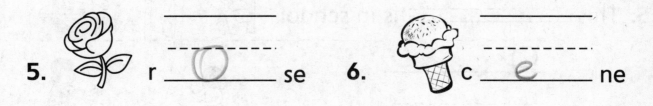

5. r __o__ se

6. c __e__ ne

Name _____

Write the word from the box that completes each sentence. Circle the picture that goes with the sentence.

ago	boy	girl	how	old	people

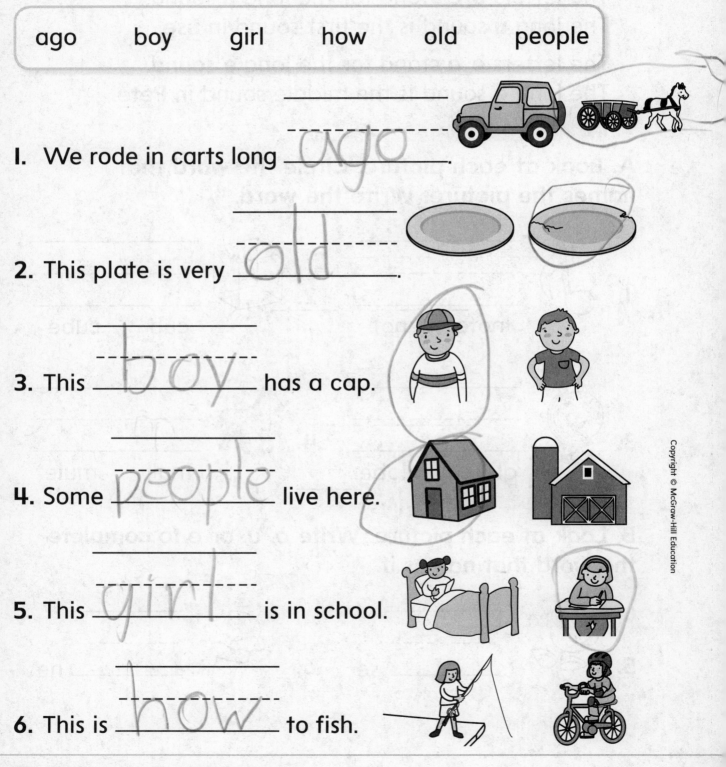

1. We rode in carts long _ago_.

2. This plate is very _old_.

3. This _boy_ has a cap.

4. Some _people_ live here.

5. This _girl_ is in school.

6. This is _how_ to fish.

Name _____

Use the words in the box to complete each sentence. Write the word on the line.

| huge | stove | Eve | these | rode | cone |

1. My name is __Eve__.

2. Pete __rode__ on his bike.

3. Its trunk is __huge__!

4. Do you like __these__ pants?

5. Put the pot on the __stove__.

6. This is a big __cone__!

Name _____

Fill in the Compare and Contrast Chart.
Use words from the story.

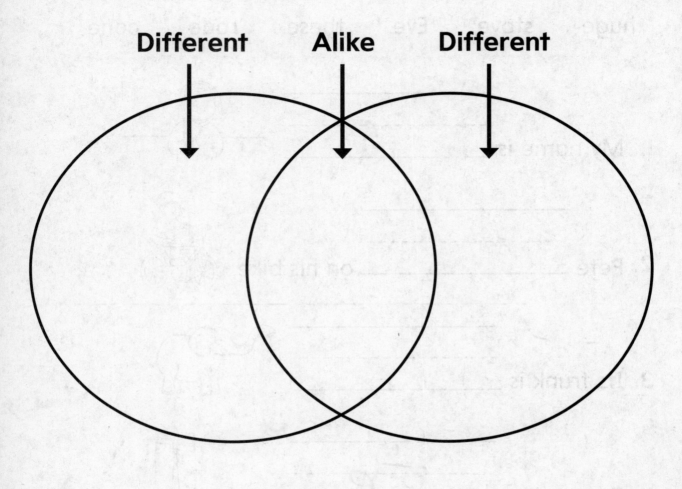

Different   **Alike**   **Different**

Life Long Ago

What was life like long ago?
What did boys and girls do?
They helped a lot at home.

①

Boys and girls still had time
to play. They had fun just
like you do!

④

Boys and girls fed the hens.
They looked for eggs.

③

Girls helped make clothes.
Boys helped to plant.

②

Name _____

Reread "Life Long Ago." Read the questions that compare and contrast what boys and girls did. Circle the words that answer each question. Write the words.

1. The boys and girls all _____.

_____
_ .

    helped   planted

2. What did girls do?

_____
_ .

Girls helped to _____.

    make clothes   read

3. What did boys do?

_____
_ .

Boys helped to _____.

    sew   plant

_____
_ .

4. Boys and girls fed the _____.

    plants   hens

Name _____

> The spellings **a_e, i_e, o_e, u_e,** and **e_e** stay together in the same syllable. The syllable usually has a long vowel sound.
>
> in/<u>side</u>   a/<u>wake</u>   <u>rose</u>/bud

Read each word. Draw a line to divide the word into syllables. Write one syllable on each line. Then circle the syllable with the long vowel sound.

1. sunshine

2. pancake

3. explode

4. handshake

5. placemat

Name _____

> **Captions** tell readers more about photos or pictures.

Look at each picture. Circle the caption that goes with the picture.

1. This is life on a farm.
   This is life in a city.

2. Horses carry goods today.
   Trucks carry goods today.

3. People rode in these long ago.
   People ride in these today.

4. People get water from a sink today.
   People got water from a well long ago.

Name _____

A. Read the draft model. Use the questions to help you add reasons to this opinion.

> ### Draft Model
>
> Games in the past were not very much fun. Games now are better. We can play games on TV.

1. What is the opinion in the writing?

2. What is a reason for the opinion?

3. What reasons could you add to the writing?

B. Now revise the draft by adding more reasons for the opinion.

_____

- -

_____

_____

- -

_____

_____

- -

_____

Name _____

> The letters **oo** and **u** can make the middle sound you hear in **book**.

Circle the word in each row that has the same middle sound you hear in too**k. Write the word.**

_____

1. hook   rope   nut   _____

2. shake   shook   stop   _____

3. fun   flop   full   _____

4. foot   tune   fudge   _____

5. rush   patch   push   _____

Name _____

Complete each sentence. Use one of the words in the box.

done	soon	every	after	work	buy

1. Matt will _____ a hat.

2. Now she is _____!

3. They will go to the park _____ school.

4. He has a lot of _____ to do.

5. There are dots on _____ sock.

6. He will wake the cat _____.

Name _____

A. Read the words in the box. Listen for the middle sound spelled <u>oo</u> or <u>u</u>. Then write each word next to a word with the same ending sounds.

> foot   pull   cook   push

1. bush   _____   **2.** soot   _____

3. book   _____   **4.** full   _____

B. Change the beginning sound in <u>good</u> to write a new word that has the same middle sound. Then write a sentence using <u>good</u> or your new word.

5. _____

_____

Name _____

Fill in the Sequence Chart. Use words from the story.

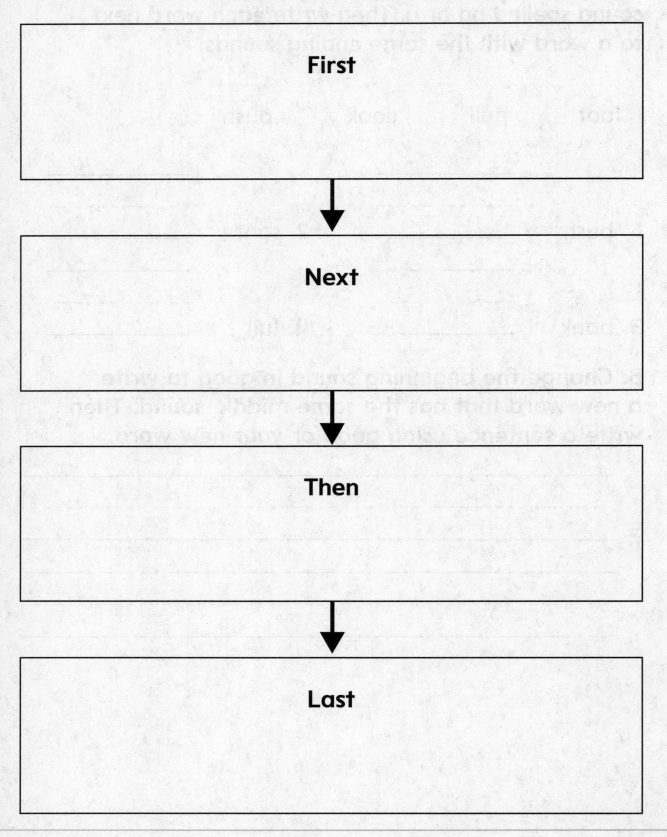

First

Next

Then

Last

④

Then we buy beans.
We cook the food.
It tastes good!

The Food We Eat

This is a big farm.
It grows beans and grapes.
Soon they can be picked.

①

After that, we go to a shop. We buy the grapes. They look good!

③

People work here. They pack up the food. Then trucks take it to shops.

②

Name _____

A. Reread "The Food We Eat." Think about what happens to the food at each stage. Answer the questions.

1. What happens to the food first?

_____

- -

_____

2. After packing, what happens to the food then?

_____

- -

_____

3. What happens to the food next?

_____

- -

_____

4. What happens to the food last?

_____

- -

_____

B. Complete the sentence to tell what the family buys.

5. The family buys

_____

- -

_____.

Name _____

> When you add **-ed** or **-ing** to the end of a word that ends with a vowel and a consonant, double the last consonant.
>
> dro**p** + ed = drop + **p** + **ed** = drop**ped**
>
> dro**p** + ing = drop + **p** + **ing** = drop**ping**

A. Add **-ed** to each word. Write the new word.

1. tag _____   2. stop _____

3. grab _____   4. slam _____

B. Add **-ing** to each word. Write the new word.

5. hug _____   6. plan _____

7. drip _____   8. skip _____

C. Write a sentence using a word you wrote above.

_____

9. _____

Name _____

> A **chart** provides information in an organized way.

**A. Use the chart to compare different foods.
Answer the questions.**

Food Colors		
Red	**Yellow**	**Green**
apple tomato _____ -------------	lemon banana _____ -------------	lime peas _____ -------------

I. Circle the two foods that are green.

    lemon   peas   lime

                      _____

                      ----

2. What color is an apple? _____

**B. Think of other foods that are red, yellow, or
green. Add their names to the chart.**

Name _____

A. Read the draft model. Use the questions to help you add more details to support the opinion.

Draft Model

It is good to grow your own food. You can grow many different plants. Then you know where your food comes from.

1. What is the opinion in the writing?

2. What detail supports the opinion?

3. What other supporting details could you add to the writing?

B. Now revise the draft by adding more details that support the opinion.

_____

- -

_____

- -

_____

- -

_____

Name _____

The letters **a**, **ai** and **ay** can make the long **a** sound.

apron   **train**   **hay**

A. Read the words in the box. Listen for the long _a_ sound. Write the word that names each picture.

| tray | snail | pail | day |

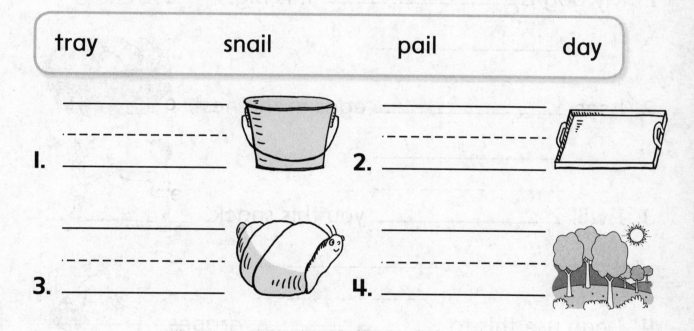

1. _____

2. _____

3. _____

4. _____

B. Write your own sentence using a word from the box.

5. _____
_____

Name _____

Complete each sentence. Use one of the words in the box.

| about | animal | carry | eight | give | our |

1. My dog is _____ this big.

2. I see _____ eggs in the nest.

3. I will _____ you this snack.

4. I can use this to _____ grapes.

5. This is _____ home.

6. A pig is an _____.

Name _____

> **special:** Something that is **special** is important or unique.
>
> **splendid:** Something that is **splendid** is wonderful or very good.

A. Match each sentence to the picture that it tells about.

1. Today is my **special** day.   **a.**

2. We had a **splendid** time on our school trip.   **b.**

B. Complete each sentence. Use a word from the word box.

> special   splendid

_____

3. The doll is _____ to me.

_____

4. Mom looks _____ in her new dress.

Name _____

Fill in the Sequence Chart. Use words from the story.

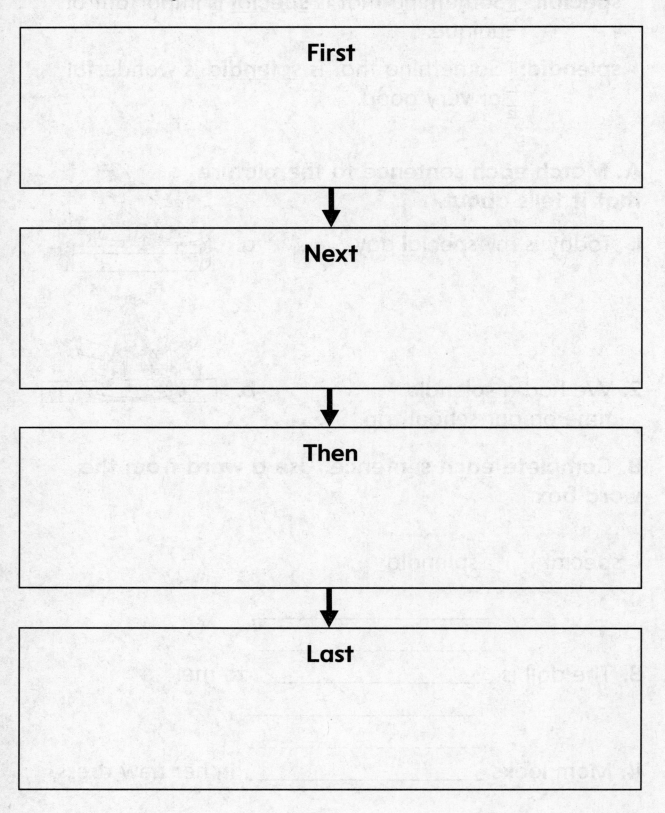

First

Next

Then

Last

He asked Hen for an egg.
"Ha!" said Hen. "You can not
trick me. I see a fox tail!"
Hen did not give Fox any eggs.

A Fox Tail

Fox wanted to eat.
"I see Hen," Fox said. "I will
get an egg from her!"

"I will trick Hen and get that egg," said Fox.
Fox dressed up. He put on a hat and old pants. He went to see Hen.

③

"May I take that egg?" Fox asked.
"No, you may not!" said Hen.

②

Name _____

A. Reread "A Fox Tail." Use the numbers to tell the order of the events.

Write 1 if the sentence and picture tell what happened first.

Write 2 if the sentence and picture tell what happened next.

Write 3 if the sentence and picture tell what happened last.

_____

1. Fox dressed up. _____

2. "I see Hen," Fox said. _____

3. "Ha!" said Hen. "You can not trick me, Fox!" _____

B. Work with a partner. Read the passage aloud. Pay attention to intonation. Stop after one minute. Fill out the chart.

	Words Read	–	Number of Errors	=	Words Correct Score
First Read		–		=	
Second Read		–		=	

Name _____

A **dictionary** is a book that gives the meanings
of words. It shows how to use a word in a sentence.

We use a **dictionary** to find out what a word means.

**A. Read the words and meanings from a
dictionary.**

special	important.
	My pup is very **special** to me.
splendid	very good.
	We had a **splendid** time with Gram.

**B. Choose the correct meaning for the word. Fill
in the circle.**

1. special   ○ important   ○ fun
2. splendid   ○ sad   ○ very good

**C. Use a word from the box to complete each
sentence.**

3. The school play was _____.

4. The gift from Mom is _____ to me.

Name _____

Read each word. Underline the letters that make the long a sound. Write the word. Circle the picture that it names.

1. train _____

2. clay _____

3. paint _____

4. apron _____

5. hay _____

Name _____

A B C D E F G H I J K L M N O P Q R S T U V W X Y Z

We put words in ABC order by looking at the first letter of each word.

<u>c</u>lay   <u>d</u>ay   <u>g</u>o

If words begin with the same letter, we look at the second letter.

b<u>a</u>t   b<u>e</u>d   b<u>o</u>x

Read the two words. Circle the word in ( ) that comes next in ABC order. Write the word.

1. pail   read   (take   stay)   _____

2. can   five   (past   gold)   _____

3. day   hive   (log   men)   _____

4. kick   loss   (make   nail)   _____

Name _____

> A **chart** gives information in an organized way.

Read the chart.

Duck	Chicken
wings	wings
long, flat beak	small beak
webbed feet	no webbed feet
lays eggs	lays eggs

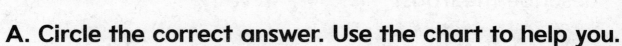

A. Circle the correct answer. Use the chart to help you.

1. Which has wings?

duck   chicken   both

2. Which has a small beak?

duck   chicken   both

3. Which has webbed feet?

duck   chicken   both

B. Use the chart to help you answer the question.

4. What is one thing that is the same about a duck and a chicken?

_____

- -

_____

Name _____

A. Read the draft model. Use the questions to help you add specific words.

> ### Draft Model
>
> Frogs have legs that are good for hopping. Frogs use their legs to jump in the water. Frogs eat bugs, too.

1. What is the topic of the writing?

2. What specific words are in the writing?

3. What other specific words could you use to describe the frogs?

B. Now revise the draft by adding more specific words to describe the frogs.

_____

_____

_____

_____

_____

_____

Name _____

The long **e** sound can be spelled with the letters **e** as in **b_e_**, **_ee_** as in **k_ee_p**, **_ea_** as in **_ea_t**, and **_ie_** as in **th_ie_f**.

Write the words from the box that have the same vowel sound and spelling.

she   sleep   each   deep   shield   seat   me   chief

1. field   _____   _____

2. eat   _____   _____

3. cheese   _____   _____

4. he   _____   _____

Name _____

Complete each sentence. Use one of the words in the box.

into	blue	or	small	other	because

_____

1. The animal is very _____ .

2. We walk _____ the school.

3. Do you want this one _____ that one?

4. I put on a hat _____ it is cold.

5. The flag is red, white, and _____ .

6. I will eat the _____ apple.

Name _____

A. Read each clue. Look at each picture. Then write a vocabulary word from the box next to the clue it goes with.

danger   partner

_____

I. The cat is not safe. _____

_____

2. We worked together. _____

B. Choose one of the vocabulary words from the box above to use in a sentence of your own. Then draw a picture to go with your sentence.

_____

3. _____

Name _____

Fill in the Main Idea and Key Details Chart. Use words from the story.

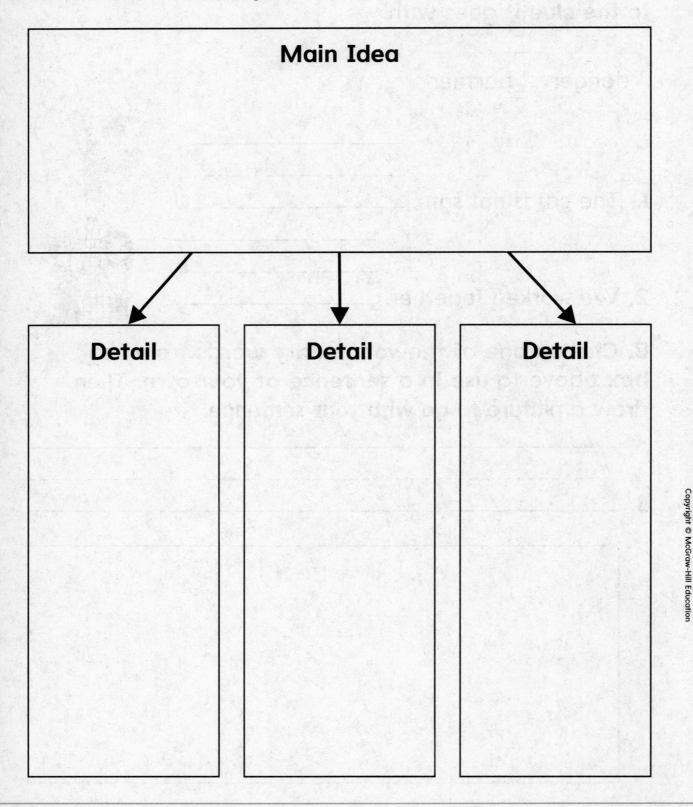

Main Idea

Detail

Detail

Detail

④

The raft of ants floats. They can wait for the rain to stop. They may reach land. Now that's teamwork!

Ants Can Help

It is raining a lot. There is water all around. How can little ants stay safe?

①

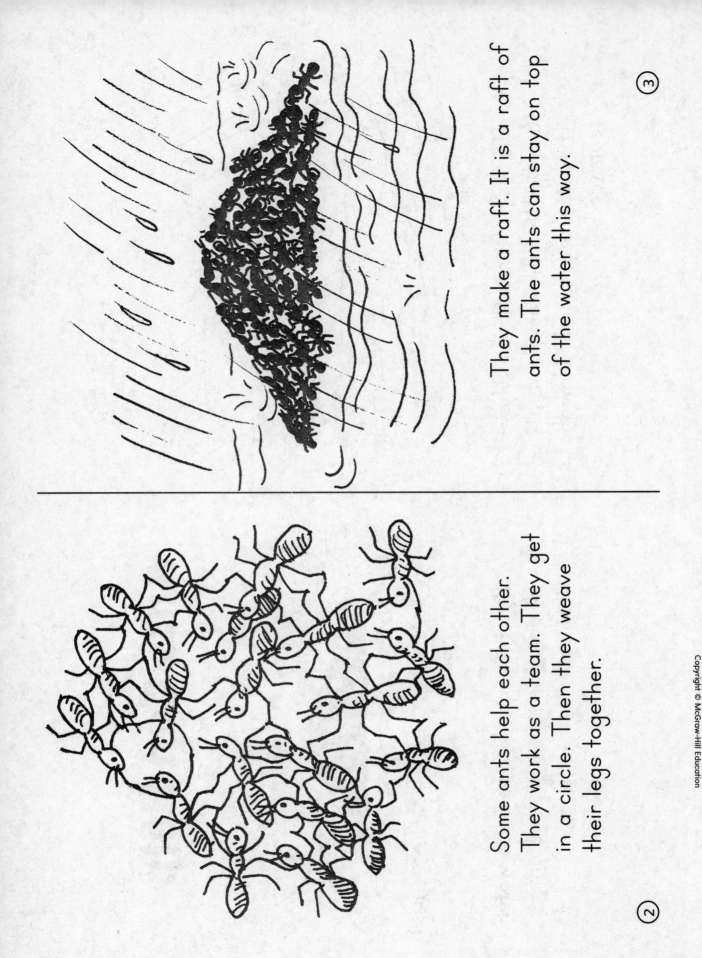

They make a raft. It is a raft of ants. The ants can stay on top of the water this way.

③

Some ants help each other. They work as a team. They get in a circle. Then they weave their legs together.

②

Name _____

A. Reread "Ants Can Help" and answer the questions.

1. What can ants do in the rain?

_____

- -

_____

2. What do the ants do with their legs?

_____

- -

_____

3. What do the ants make?

_____

- -

_____

4. How do the ants stay safe?

_____

- -

_____

B. Work with a partner. Read the passage aloud. Pay attention to appropriate phrasing. Stop after one minute. Fill out the chart.

	Words Read	–	Number of Errors	=	Words Correct Score
First Read		–		=	
Second Read		–		=	

Name _____

> **Context clues** are words that help you figure out the meaning of a new word. When you see a new word, look for words you know to help you.

Use context clues to figure out the meaning of the word in bold. Fill in the correct circle.

1. The lions sit and **relax** on the grass.

   ○ rest

   ○ run

2. Lee **enjoys** seeing the lions. He has a fun time.

   ○ likes

   ○ looks

3. The **timid** lion hid behind his mother.

   ○ shy

   ○ happy

Name _____

Read the word. Draw a line under the letters that make the long e sound. Write the letters on the line. Circle the matching picture.

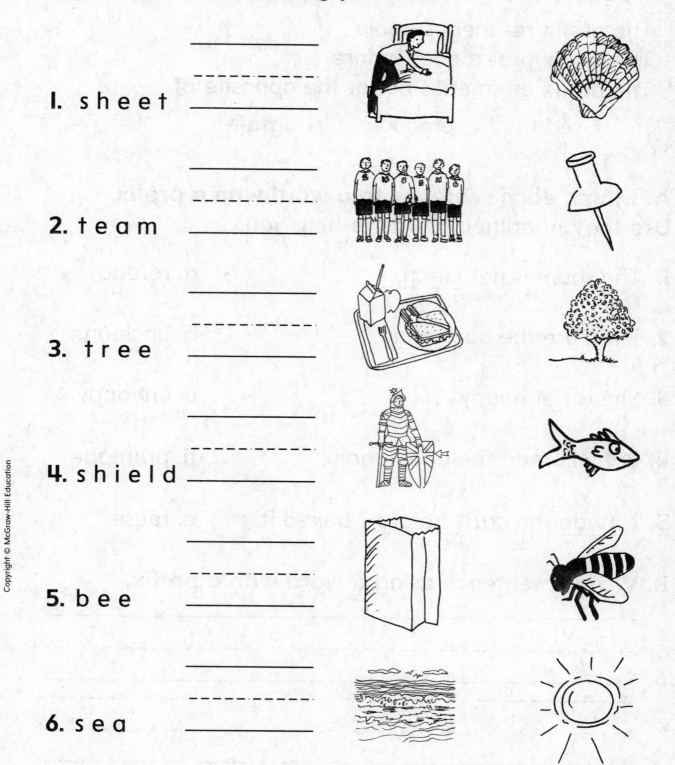

1. s h e e t _____

2. t e a m _____

3. t r e e _____

4. s h i e l d _____

5. b e e _____

6. s e a _____

Name _____

A **prefix** is a word part you can add to the beginning of a word to change its meaning.

The prefix **re-** means **again**.
The prefix **pre-** means **before**.
The prefix **un-** means **not** or **the opposite of**.

<u>re</u>do   <u>pre</u>cook   <u>un</u>safe

**A. Match each sentence to a word with a prefix.
Use the underlined words to help you.**

1. The room is <u>not clean</u>.   **a.** reread

2. I will <u>use</u> the bag <u>again</u>.   **b.** unclean

3. She is <u>not happy</u>.   **c.** unhappy

4. Pat will <u>read</u> the book <u>again</u>.   **d.** premade

5. I <u>made</u> the crust <u>before</u> I baked it.   **e.** reuse

B. Write a sentence using a word with a prefix.

_____

- -

6. _____

_____

- -

_____

Name _____

Captions are short descriptions that tell more about a photograph or picture.

A. Circle the caption that tells about the picture.

1. Honey is sweet.
   Bees make honey.

2. A grasshopper can hop.
   An ant is very little.

3. Some bugs live in trees.
   Ants can walk in a line.

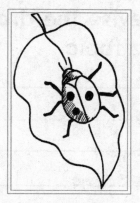

4. Ladybugs have spots.
   Spiders have eight legs.

B. Choose a picture. Write another caption.

5. _____

Name _____

A. Read the draft model. Use the questions to help you add a topic to the writing.

> ### Draft Model
>
> Some fish help each other find food. Sometimes dogs team up to take care of their puppies. Zebras and wildebeests help keep each other safe in the wild.

1. Does the writing tell what the topic is?

2. What do the sentences tell about?

3. What sentence could you add at the beginning to tell the topic?

B. Now revise the draft by adding a sentence about the topic.

Name _____

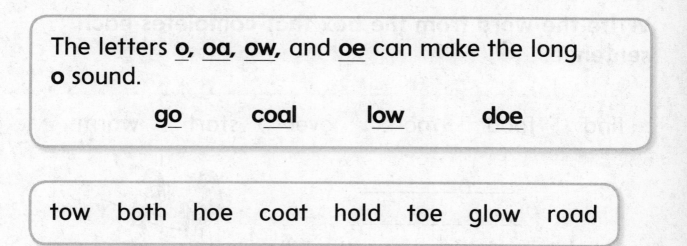

The letters <u>o</u>, <u>oa</u>, <u>ow</u>, and <u>oe</u> can make the long o sound.

go   coal   low   doe

tow   both   hoe   coat   hold   toe   glow   road

Write the words from the box that have the same vowel sound and spelling.

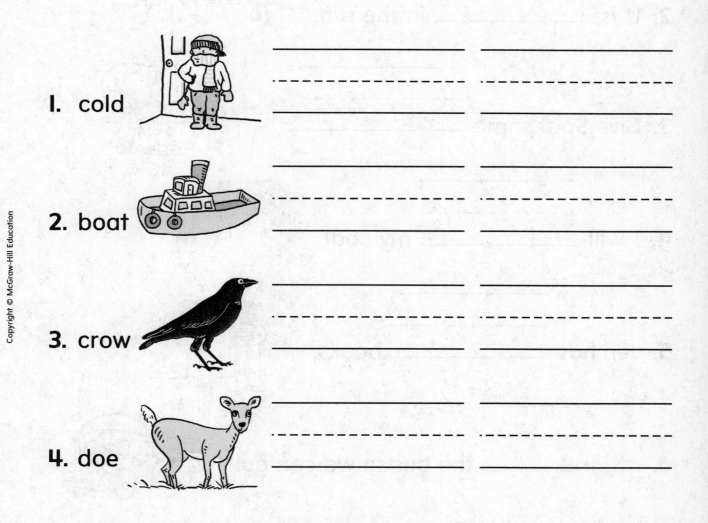

I. cold

2. boat

3. crow

4. doe

Name _____

Write the word from the box that completes each sentence.

find	food	more	over	start	warm

1. We hike _____ the hill.

2. It is _____ in the sun.

3. Give Spot some _____ .

4. I will _____ my coat.

5. Jen has _____ books.

6. _____ the bus so we can go!

Name _____

You can use the words **seek** and **search** to tell about looking for something.

Use **search** to tell about looking for something in a place.

Use **seek** to tell about looking for something you want.

Circle the word that best completes the sentence. Write the word on the line.

_____

- - - - - - - - - - - - - - - - - -

1. Kim has to _____ the closet for her coat.

    search   seek

_____

- - - - - - - - - - - - - - - - - -

2. The crow must _____ out food.

    search   seek

_____

- - - - - - - - - - - - - - - - - -

3. The prince will _____ a princess.

    search   seek

_____

- - - - - - - - - - - - - - - - - -

4. I will _____ my desk for a pencil.

    seek   search

Name _____

Fill in the Main Idea and Key Details Chart. Use words from the story.

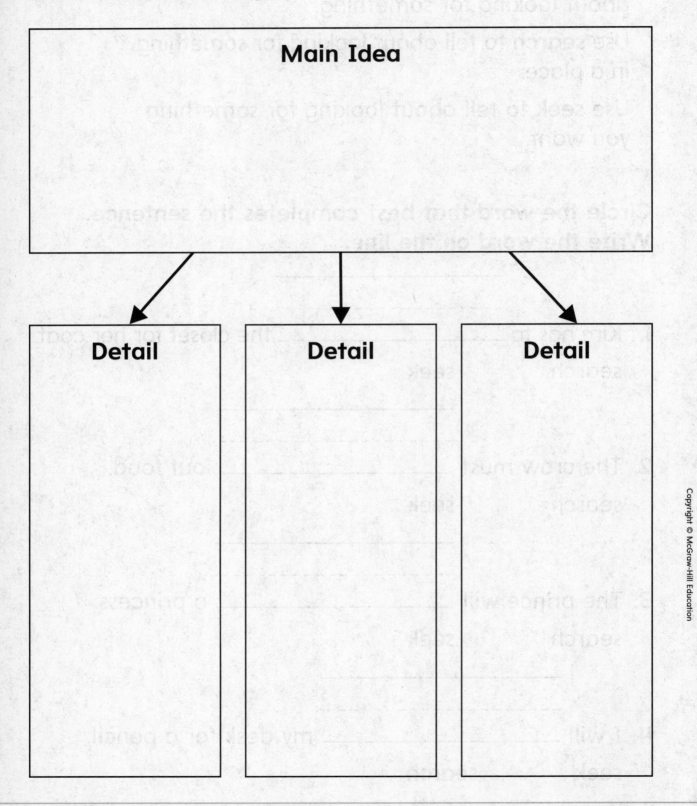

Main Idea

Detail

Detail

Detail

Can a crow be bold? Yes! It likes to take things. This crow brings a shell back to its nest!

④

Crows

Have you seen a crow? Crows are big. They are mostly black. They live in many places.

①

Crows make nests. They made this nest from sticks. The top is open.

What does a crow eat? Crows eat what they can find. It could be ants, crops, or bugs. They even eat eggs and fish.

③

②

Name _____

A. Reread "Crows." Then answer the questions.

I. Key details tell you more about the main idea. You can find key details in the words or in photos and illustrations. What is a key detail you read?

_____

- -

_____

2. What is one more key detail you read?

_____

- -

_____

3. The main idea of a selection is what it is mainly about. What is the main idea of "Crows"?

_____

- -

_____

B. Work with a partner. Read the passage aloud. Pay attention to expression. Stop after one minute. Fill out the chart.

	Words Read	–	Number of Errors	=	Words Correct Score
First Read		–		=	
Second Read		–		=	

Name _____

A **word category** is a group of words that are alike in some way.

Word Category: **Things People Do**

learn, eat, sleep, play

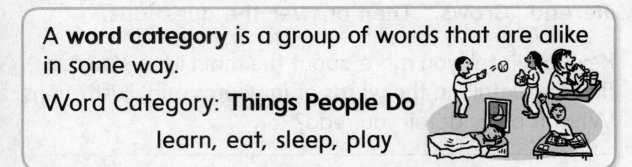

A. Reread "Crows." Then look for words that fit each category. Write the missing word.

_____

- - - - - - - - - - - -

1. Things Crows Eat: ants, crops, _____

_____

- - - - - - - - - - - -

2. Things Crows Do: _____, make nests, eat

B. Write a word category that tells how the words in each group are alike.

Word Category:

_____

- - - - - - - - - - - - - - -

3. wings, beak, legs, feet _____

_____

- - - - - - - - - - - - - - -

4. dogs, cats, birds, fish _____

Name _____

Use the words in the box to complete the sentences.

| coat | show | boat | row | toe | go |

1. They put on a _____.

2. We can _____ fast.

3. Put on your _____.

4. We sit in the same _____.

5. I hit my big _____.

Name _____

An **open syllable** is a syllable that ends in a vowel. It has a long vowel sound.

ro/bot   ho/tel

Read each word. Draw a line between the syllables in each word. Write the word that has an open syllable.

1. begin   picnic   _____

2. inside   silent   _____

3. magnet   locate   _____

4. retell   escape   _____

5. sunset   beneath   _____

6. pilot   pancake   _____

Name _____

> Some words help readers see, hear, feel, taste or smell. These words are called **sensory words**.

Read the sentence. Underline the sensory word. Write the word on the line.

_____

– – – – – – – – – – – – –

1. The day is sunny. _____

_____

– – – – – – – – – – – –

2. A loud truck went down the street. _____

_____

– – – – – – – – – – – –

3. I pat the fluffy chick. _____

_____

– – – – – – – – – –

4. The cake has creamy frosting. _____

_____

– – – – – – – – – –

5. The garden smelled sweet. _____

_____

– – – – – – – – – –

6. I clean up the sticky mess. _____

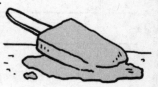

Name _____

A. Read the draft model. Use the questions to help you add a topic to the writing.

> ### Draft Model
>
> Songbirds fly to find food and look for seeds to eat. Dogs use their great noses to smell and find where the food is. Cats like to hunt for their food.

1. Does the writing tell about a topic?

2. What do the sentences tell about?

3. What sentence could you add to tell the topic?

B. Now revise the draft by adding a sentence about the topic.

_____

_____

_____

_____

Name _____

> The long **i** sound is the sound you hear in the middle of **wild**. The letters **i**, **y**, **igh**, and **ie** can stand for the long **i** sound.
>
> **find**   **sky**   **night**   **tie**

A. Circle the long i word that completes each sentence. Write the word.

I. The baby will _____.

cry   sips

2. We like _____.

cake   pie

3. The sun is out so there is a lot of _____.

light   dim

B. Write i, y, igh, or ie to complete the word that names each picture.

4. w ___ l d   5. f l ___

Name _____

Write the word from the box that completes each sentence.

caught	flew	know	laugh	listen	were

_____

1. He _____ a bug.

_____

2. I _____ at jokes.

_____

3. The butterfly _____ away.

_____

4. They _____ playing in mud.

_____

5. We must _____ in school.

_____

6. Do you _____ where bees live?

Name _____

A. Write a sentence that uses the word <u>beautiful</u>. Then draw a picture to go with your sentence.

_____
- -
_____
_____
- -
_____

B. Write a sentence that uses the word <u>fancy</u>. Then draw a picture to go with your sentence.

_____
- -
_____
_____
- -
_____

Name _____

Fill in the Point of View Chart. Use words from the story.

Character	Clue	Point of View

Eve and Pete

Eve and Pete slept in the tree.
One warm day, the bugs woke up.
It was spring! So Eve and Pete said
good-bye. They flew up to the sky.

④

Eve and Pete were pals.
They flew and flew high and low.
They had so much fun together.

①

They spotted a huge tree. There were lots of bugs inside.

"Hi! Stay with us," the bugs cried. "You will be warm here."

③

Then one day, Pete said, "It's getting cold. We need to find a tree. We need to sleep."

"Let's look for one," said Eve.

②

Name _____

A. Reread "Eve and Pete."
Circle the words that answer
each question. Write the words.

1. The story characters are _____.

    bugs   trees

2. Pete said they needed to _____.

    sleep   play

3. The bugs said _____.

    stay with us   go away

4. When spring came, Eve and Pete

    _____

    stayed   flew away

B. Work with a partner. Read the passage aloud.
Use appropriate phrasing. Stop after one minute.

	Words Read	–	Number of Errors	=	Words Correct Score
First Read		–		=	
Second Read		–		=	

Name _____

> **Context clues** are words that help you figure out the meaning of a new word. Look for context clues in the same sentence or in nearby sentences.

Use context clues to figure out the meaning of the word in bold. Fill in the circle next to the word's meaning.

1. There are many kinds of bugs, but all **insects** have six legs.

   ○ bugs

   ○ legs

2. Most spiders are **harmless** and won't hurt you.

   ○ safe

   ○ dangerous

3. Some caterpillars have **bristles,** or short hairs.

   ○ eyes

   ○ hairs

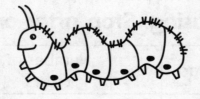

Name _____

Circle the word in each group that has the long <u>i</u> sound. Write the word.

I. child   chill   chip

2. twist   tie   thin

3. ring   rip   right

4. drip   dry   dig

5. mist   mitt   might

6. bright   bring   bits

Name _____

To add the ending -**es** or -**ed** to a word that ends
with long **i** spelled **y**, first change the **y** to **i**.

> **dry + es = dries**   **dry + ed = dried**

Do not change the **y** to **i** when adding -**ing**.

> **dry + ing = drying**

Add the ending to the word. Write the new word.

1. spy + ed   =   _____

2. fly + ing   =   _____

3. cry + es   =   _____

4. try + ed   =   _____

5. fry + ing   =   _____

6. try + es   =   _____

Name _____

> A **heading** tells readers what information is in a section of a text.

Read the text. Follow the directions.

Honeybees

A. In a Bee Hive
  Honeybees live in a hive. There are many rooms in the hive. The rooms are made from wax. Bees store food in the wax rooms.

B. Most bees in the hive are worker bees. Worker bees fly to flowers. They get sweet nectar. Bees eat some of the nectar. They make the rest into honey.

I. What is the article about? Circle the answer.

spiders   honeybees   insects

2. Circle a heading in the text.

3. The heading for section B is missing. Write a heading on the line.

_____

- -

_____

Name _____

A. Read the draft model. Use the questions to help you add a concluding statement.

> ### Draft Model
>
> Ants are small but they are strong. They work together to build hills around their tunnels. A team of ants can move a large bug or leaf.

1. What is the topic of the writing?

2. What details tell about the topic?

3. What information could you include in a concluding statement?

B. Now revise the draft by adding a strong conclusion to sum up the writing and tell the main idea.

_____

_____

_____

_____

_____

_____

Name _____

> The letters **y** and **<u>ey</u>** at the end of a word can make the long **e** sound.
>
> ### ba**b<u>y</u>**   val**l<u>ey</u>**

Write **y** or **<u>ey</u>** on the line. Then write the word.

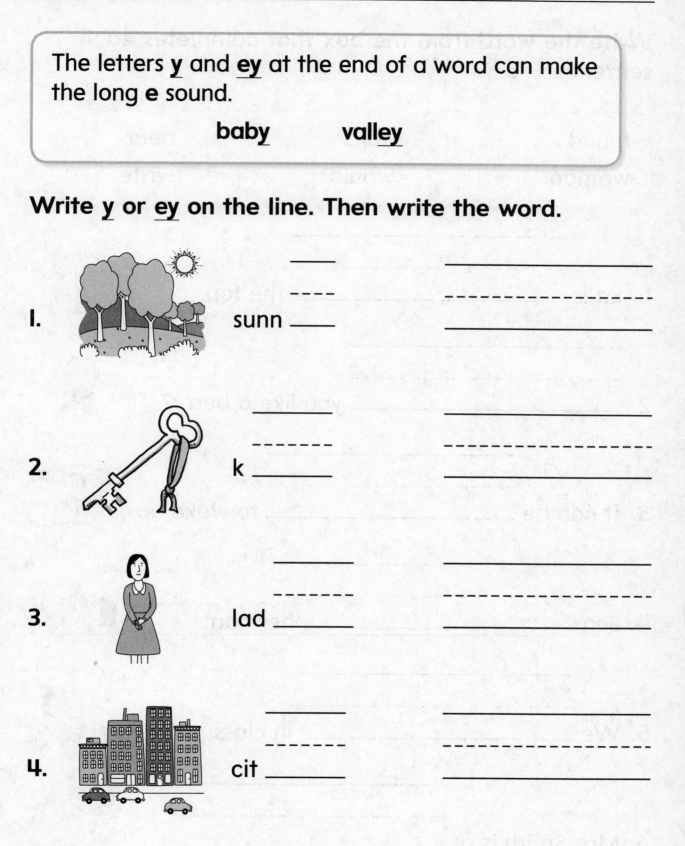

1. sunn _____ _____

2. k _____ _____

3. lad _____ _____

4. cit _____ _____

Name _____

Write the word from the box that completes each sentence.

found	hard	near
woman	would	write

_____

1. Ed is _____ the top.

_____

2. _____ you like a berry?

_____

3. It can be _____ to wake up.

_____

4. Jen _____ her coat.

_____

5. We _____ in class.

_____

6. Mrs. Smith is a _____.

Name _____

A person who is **clever** thinks of good ideas quickly.

The clever girl found the answer to the riddle.

When you see or hear a **signal**, it is time to do something.

A teacher will give a signal to line up for gym class.

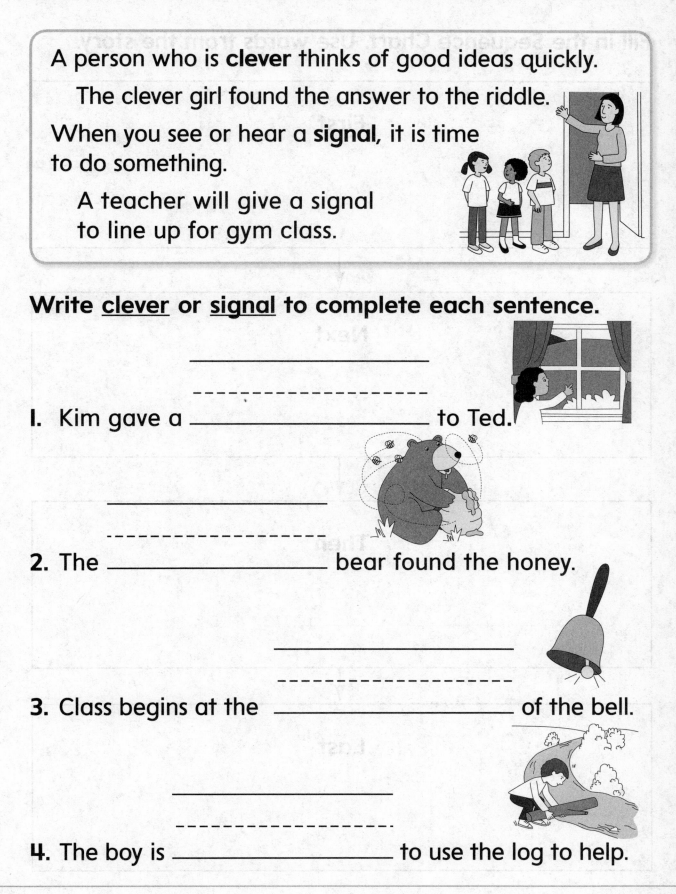

Write <u>clever</u> or <u>signal</u> to complete each sentence.

_____

- - - - - - - - - - - - - - - -

I. Kim gave a _____ to Ted.

_____

- - - - - - - - - - - - - -

2. The _____ bear found the honey.

_____

- - - - - - - - - - - - - - - -

3. Class begins at the _____ of the bell.

_____

- - - - - - - - - - - - - -

4. The boy is _____ to use the log to help.

Name _____

Fill in the Sequence Chart. Use words from the story.

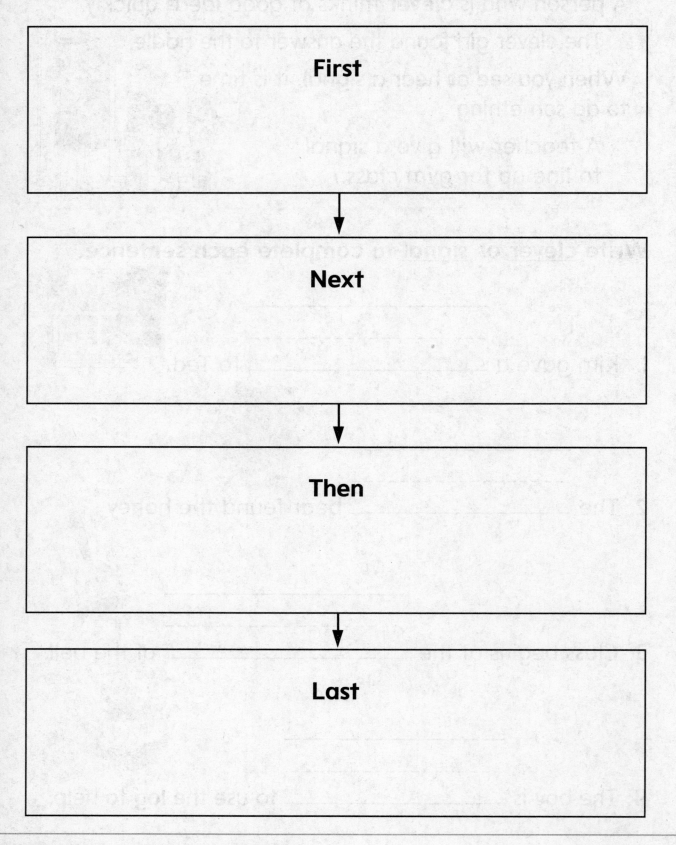

First

Next

Then

Last

(4)

Hold a treat near its nose.
Then say, "Sit!" Do it many times.
What will the puppy do?
It just might sit!

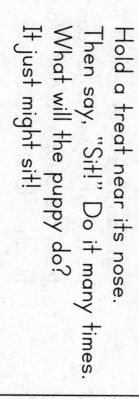

A New Puppy

Animal Shelter

Would you like a puppy? You can
find one here. They are all so
cute. The woman can help you
pick the right one.

(1)

Puppy Classes

You can take it to school or train it at home. What can you train the puppy to do? You can teach it to sit.

③

Animal Shelter

You find a puppy. Now you bring it home. Having a puppy is hard work. Why? First, you must train it. It is not easy.

②

Name _____

A. Reread "A New Puppy." Think about what happens in the selection. Order the steps from 1 to 4.

_____

- - - - - - -

_____ You train the puppy.

_____

- - - - - - -

_____ You find a puppy. You take it home.

_____

- - - - - - -

_____ You look for a puppy.

_____

- - - - - - -

_____ The puppy learns to sit.

B. Work with a partner. Read the passage aloud. Pay attention to intonation. Stop after one minute. Fill out the chart.

	Words Read	–	Number of Errors	=	Words Correct Score
First Read		–		=	
Second Read		–		=	

Name _____

> A **root word** is a word that can stand alone. You can add letters to a root word to make a new word.
>
> **look + ed = <u>look</u>ed**   **look + ing = <u>look</u>ing**
>
> When you see a new word, look for a root word to help you figure out the meaning.

Read the word. Write the root word on the line.

1. filling _____

2. spilled _____

3. playing _____

4. cleaned _____

5. cooking _____

Name _____

Use the words in the box to complete the sentences.

easy	money	happy	tidy	honey

_____

----

1. I am _____ that you can help me write.

_____

----

2. Bees make _____.

_____

----

3. It's not _____ to clean our dog!

_____

----

4. My desk is neat and _____.

_____

----

5. It costs _____ to ride the bus.

Name _____

> A **compound word** is made up of smaller words.
>
> rain + coat = raincoat

A. Add a word from the box to a word below to make a compound word. Write the word from the box. Then read the compound word.

> | walk | time | work | book |
> | --- | --- | --- | --- |

1. home _____

2. lunch _____

3. side _____

4. note _____

B. Circle the compound word. Then draw a line between the two smaller words.

5. someone   singing

6. silly   inside

7. backpack   unpack

8. basket   baseball

9. floppy   flagpole

Name _____

> **Captions** tell readers more about photographs or pictures.

Look at each picture. Read the caption. Use the picture and caption to answer the question.

Some birds build
nests in trees.

I. **Which builds nests in trees? Circle the answer.**
   birds   cats   dogs

Jan and Dad
like to fish.

2. **What do Jan and Dad like to do? Write the answer.**

_____

- - - - - - - - - - - - - - - - - - - -

_____

Cats and dogs
can get along.

3. **Which two animals can get along? Circle the answer.**
   cats   dogs   frogs

Name _____

A. Read the draft model. Use the questions to help you add time-order words.

> ### Draft Model
>
> A puppy is chosen to be a guide dog. The puppy learns special tasks like how to carry things or walk with someone who cannot see. The puppy goes to live with someone who needs help.

I. What is the topic of the writing?

2. What happens first? What happens next?

3. What time-order words could you add to make the writing more clear?

B. Now revise the draft by adding time-order words to make the writing more clear.

_____

_____

_____

_____

_____

_____

_____

Name _____

> The letters <u>ar</u> together make the sounds
> you hear at the end of c<u>ar</u>.

**Read the words in the box. Listen for the <u>ar</u> sounds.
Write the word that names each picture.**

> scarf   arm   shark   star

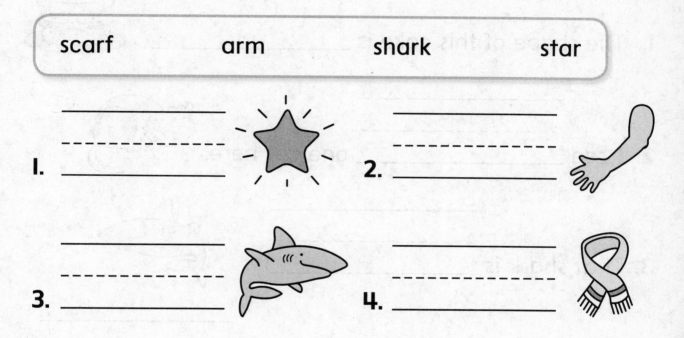

1. _____

2. _____

3. _____

4. _____

**Write your own sentence using a word from
the box.**

5. _____

_____

_____

Name _____

Complete each sentence. Use one of the words in the box.

four	none	only	large	put	round

1. The shape of this cake is _____.

2. I see _____ one cat here.

3. That shark is _____!

4. Carl wants an apple, but there are _____.

5. There are _____ swings.

6. I can help _____ the dishes in the sink.

Name _____

> **trouble:** If you have <u>**trouble**</u> doing something, you have problems doing it.
>
> **whole:** When something is <u>**whole**</u>, it is complete. None of it is missing.

A. Match each sentence to the picture that it tells about.

1. I had trouble cleaning my room.

    a.

2. We will eat the whole cake.

    b.

B. Complete each sentence. Use a word from the word box.

> trouble   whole

_____

3. Mom had _____ with the car today.

_____

4. He ate half his snack and I ate my _____ snack.

Name _____

Fill in the Point of View Chart. Use words from the story.

Character	Clue	Point of View

④

Then the pals went for a swim.
"You are great pals!" said Cat.
They had fun, fun, fun in the sun!

The Party

"I am six today," laughed Cat.
"Let's have a party."
"Let's have it at the beach,"
said her pals. "It is not far."

①

The four pals went to the beach.
They put on party hats. They ate
cake. Cat opened her gift and
card.

③

"I will bring hats!," said Pig.
"I will bake a cake!" said Dog.
"I will make a gift and card!"
said Chick.

②

Name _____

A. Reread "The Party." Think about each character's point of view. Answer the questions.

I. Why did Cat want to have a party?

_____

- -

_____ .

2. How can you tell Dog, Pig, and Chick want to have a party?

_____

- -

_____ .

3. Did the pals like the party? How can you tell?

_____

- -

_____ .

B. Work with a partner. Read the passage aloud. Pay attention to fluency. Stop after one minute.

	Words Read	–	Number of Errors	=	Words Correct Score
First Read		–		=	
Second Read		–		=	

Name _____

Some words have more than one meaning.

bark   part of a tree

bark   a sound a dog makes

My dog likes to **bark** at trucks.

The word <u>dog</u> is a clue to help you know the correct meaning of **bark** in this sentence.

Read each sentence. Fill in the circle next to the picture that shows the correct meaning of the bold word. Use other words in the sentence to help you.

1. We will see a **play** today.

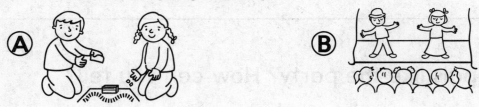

2. I **left** my lunch on the seat of the bus.

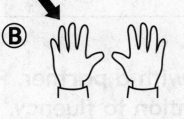

3. Let's **seal** the box and then mail it.

Name _____

Read the sentence. Circle the word that completes each sentence. Write the word on the line.

_____

- - - - - - - - - - - - - - - - - -

1. I got a _____ in the mail today.

   card   car

_____

- - - - - - - - - - - - - - - - - -

2. A _____ can swim fast.

   shark   sharp

_____

- - - - - - - - - - - - - - - - - -

3. The ducks and hens live on a _____.

   far   farm

_____

- - - - - - - - - - - - - - - - - -

4. I saw a pig near the _____.

   barn   bark

_____

- - - - - - - - - - - - - - - - - -

5. We can swing and play in the _____.

   park   part

Name _____

We add -<u>s</u> or -<u>es</u> to make some words mean "more than one."

farm ⟶ farm<u>s</u>   marsh ⟶ marsh<u>es</u>

Some words change in other ways to mean "more than one."

man ⟶ men   child ⟶ children

Some words do not change to mean "more than one."

sheep ⟶ sheep

Circle the correct word to complete the sentence. Write the word.

_____

1. The five _____ ran away.

mouses   mice

_____

2. All the _____ went to the park.

children   childs

_____

3. A shark has many sharp _____.

tooths   teeth

Name _____

A **photograph** or an **illustration** is a picture that gives information about a nonfiction text. Look at photographs and illustrations to find facts and details.

A. Look at the illustration. Circle the sentence that tells a detail about the illustration.

They sit in the shade.

They put on coats.

B. Look at the illustration again. Write a sentence that tells another detail about the illustration.

_____

- -

_____

- -

_____

Name _____

A. Read the draft model. Use the questions to help you make all of the sentences complete.

> ### Draft Model
>
> I like fruits and vegetables. Apples and bananas the most. Sometimes carrots and kale.

1. What is the topic of the writing?

2. Which sentence is complete?

3. Which sentences are incomplete?

B. Now revise the draft by correcting the incomplete sentences.

_____

_____

_____

_____

_____

_____

Name _____

> The end sound you hear in **fur** can be spelled **er** as in **her**, **ir** as in **dirt**, **ur** as in **turn**, and **or** as in **word**.

A. Read the words. Listen for the sound at the end of fur. Circle the word that names the picture.

1. wide   worm

2. bed   bird

3. shirt   show

4. sun   surf

B. Use a word from the box to complete each sentence.

> her   nurse   skirt   work

_____

5. There is a _____ at my school.

_____

6. _____ hat is green.

_____

7. I have a pretty blue _____.

Name _____

Draw a line to match the sentence to the picture it describes.

1. Can I have **another** cup of water?

    a.

2. My bag is **full** of food.

    b.

3. The boy will **climb** up the tree.

    c.

4. We walk **through** the door at school.

    d.

5. The **poor** girl is sick.

    e.

6. That kite is **great**.

    f.

Name _____

> **Leaped** means to have jumped far.
>
> **Stretched** means to have extended a body part.

A. Use a word from the box to finish each sentence.

> leaped   stretched

_____
- -

I. Millie _____ her arms to her mom.

_____
- -

2. The frog _____ across the pond.

B. Write a sentence using a word from the box. Draw a picture to go with your sentence.

_____
- -

3. _____
- -

_____

Name _____

Fill in the Cause and Effect Chart. Use events from the story.

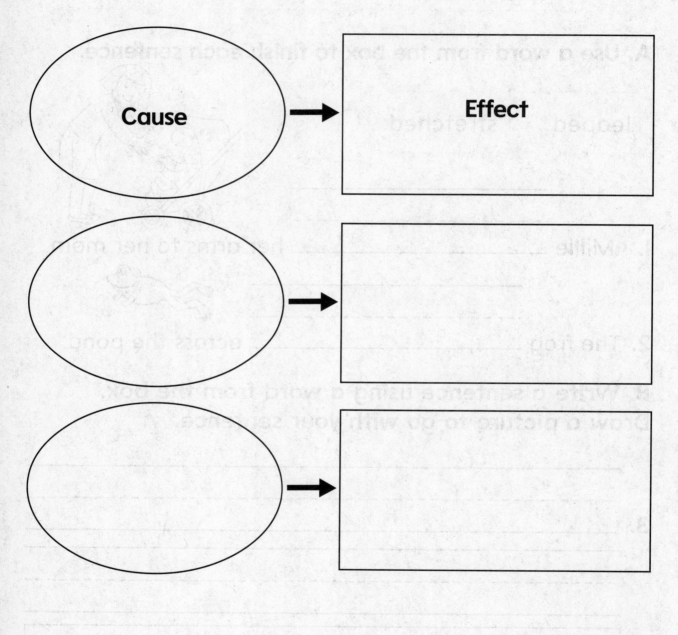

④

"That wishing star worked,"
said Bethy. She put on her hat.
"It's my turn next," said Freddy.
"Good!" said Bethy.

A Bunny Wish

"There's a wishing star!" Bethy
Bunny said to Freddy Frog. "I
wish for a sunhat!"
They were going to the beach
the next day.

①

The next day Freddy brought
Bethy a sun hat.
"Oh, my wish came true!"
exclaimed Bethy.

③

"I think you will get your wish,"
said Freddy Frog.
"I think I will, too," said Bethy.

②

Name _____

A. Reread "A Bunny Wish." Follow the directions.

1. What causes Bethy to make a wish?

_____

- -

2. Write the word that tells you what Bethy wishes for.

_____

- - - - - - - - - - - - - - - -

_____

3. What effect does Bethy's wish have?

_____

- -

_____

4. What causes Bethy to want a sunhat?

_____

- -

_____

B. Work with a partner. Read the passage aloud. Pay attention to intonation. Stop after one minute. Fill out the chart.

	Words Read	–	Number of Errors	=	Words Correct Score
First Read		–		=	
Second Read		–		=	

Name _____

> **Shades of meaning** are small differences in meaning between similar words.

Read the sentences. Then choose the best word in bold to answer the question.

1. Max is very wet. Is Max **soaked** or **damp**?

_____

- -

_____

2. Tess is giving the dog some food.
   Is Tess **pouring** or **spilling** the food?

_____

- -

_____

3. Kate thinks the party is great.
   Does Kate think the party is **good** or **wonderful**?

_____

- -

_____

Name _____

Circle the word that completes the sentence.
Then write the word.

_____

----

1. The _____ is in the nest.

    bag   bird

_____

----

2. The bird will eat the _____.

    wave   worm

_____

----

3. Nan _____ her foot.

    hut   hurt

_____

----

4. I won _____ place!

    first   fish

_____

----

5. He gave a gift to _____.

    her   harp

Name _____

> Adding -**er** to an action word changes the word to a
> naming word.
>
> teach + **er** = **teacher**   work + **er** = **worker**
>
> a person who teaches   a person who works

A. Add -er to the action word to make a naming word. Write the new word.

_____

l. play + er = _____

_____

2. help + er = _____

_____

3. paint + er = _____

_____

4. surf + er = _____

B. Write your own sentence. Use a naming word you wrote above.

_____

5. _____

Name _____

> **Captions** are short descriptions that tell more about a photograph or picture.

Circle the caption that tells about the picture.

1. Dad and Jess look at the moon.

Dad and Jess read about the moon.

2. The spaceship is near the moon.

The spaceship landed.

3. He is on the spaceship.

He is on the moon.

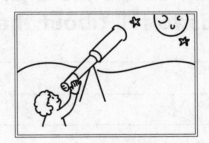

4. Dan looks at the moon.

Dan looks at a map.

5. They like to read.

They gaze at the stars.

6. They have moon rocks.

They look up at the moon.

Name _____

A. Read the draft model. Use the questions to help you add describing words.

Draft Model

I like to look at the night sky with my dad. There is a lot to see in the sky. There are stars in the sky.

---

1. What is the topic of the writing?

2. What describing word is used in the writing?

3. What describing words could you add to the writing?

B. Now revise the draft by adding describing words to tell about the night sky.

_____

_____

_____

_____

_____

_____

_____

Name _____

> The letters **or**, **ore**, and **oar** make the sounds you hear in **for**, m**ore**, and b**oar**d.

Circle the word that answers the riddle. Then underline the letters that spell the or sounds as in for, more, or board.

1. You need to buy things.

Where do you go?　　store　　star

2. I put on my hat.

What did I do?　　give　　wore

3. There is rain and wind!

What is it?　　storm　　steam

4. We go out and see new things.

What do we do?　　explore　　bore

5. Leo spoke!

What did Leo do?　　fetch　　roar

Name _____

Use a word from the box to complete each sentence.

began	better	guess	learn	right	sure

1. Can you _____ what is in the box?

2. I am _____ I will do well on my test.

3. Mom _____ to cut the cake.

4. We will _____ how to plant a tree.

5. I like this book _____ than that one.

6. This is the _____ way to ride a bike.

Name _____

An **idea** is a picture you see in your head.
I have a good idea for a story.

Something that is **unusual** is not common.
What an unusual hat you have!

Write <u>idea</u> or <u>unusual</u> to complete each sentence.

_____

1. Dan has an _____ for fixing the vase.

_____

2. That is an _____ house.

_____

3. It was a very _____ day.

_____

4. I have an _____ for a game we can play.

Name _____

Fill in the Problem and Solution Chart. Use words from the story.

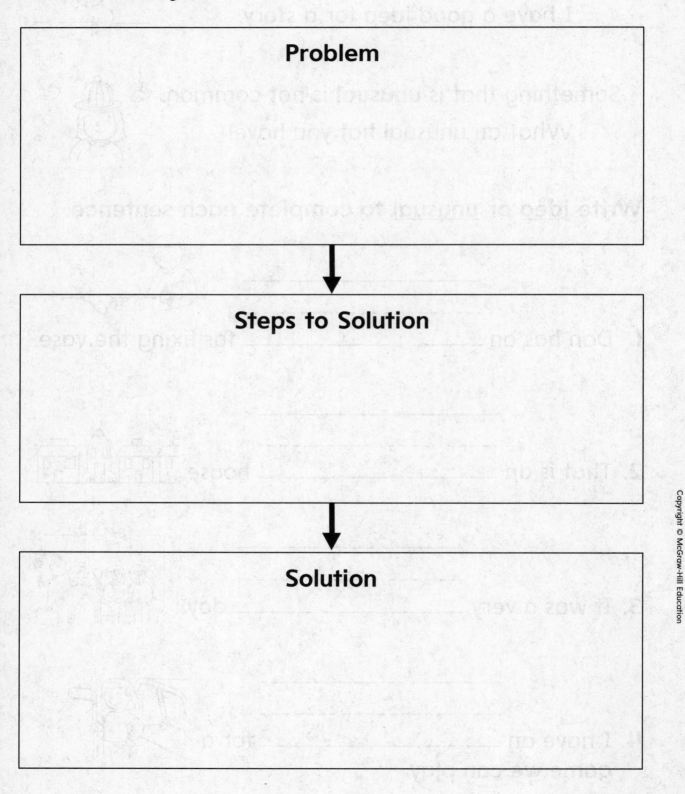

Problem

Steps to Solution

Solution

④

KK made some changes. The cuff worked much better than before. Soon lots of people wore her cuff. KK's idea was a hit!

Good Ideas

Anyone can invent! Ben Franklin invented a stove and glasses. But even kids can invent. Here is one true story.

①

KK had a good idea. She made a fleece cuff. But it did not work too well. It still let snow in.

③

KK liked winter. She liked to play outside. But her hands got so cold in the snow. She wanted to spend more time in the snow.

②

Name _____

Reread "Good Ideas." Then write "problem" or "solution" next to each sentence.

_____
- - - - - - - - - - - - - - - - - -

1. KK's hands get cold in the winter. _____

_____
- - - - - - - - - - - - - - - - - -

2. KK made a cuff. _____

_____
- - - - - - - - - - - - - - - - - -

3. The cuff did not work well. _____

_____
- - - - - - - - - - - - - - - - - -

4. KK made a better cuff. _____

B. Work with a partner. Read the passage aloud. Pay attention to appropriate phrasing. Stop after one minute. Fill out the chart.

	Words Read	–	Number of Errors	=	Words Correct Score
First Read		–		=	
Second Read		–		=	

Name _____

> A **prefix** is a word part added to the beginning of a word. A prefix changes the meaning of the word.
>
> The prefix **re-** means "again": **re** + read = **re**read
>
> **Re**read means "to read again."
>
> The prefix **un-** means "not": **un** + **real** = **un**real
>
> **Un**real means "not real."

A. Add the prefix to the word. Write the new word on the line. Then match the new word to a picture.

1. re + write = _____

2. un + tied = _____

B. Add re- or un- to a word in the box to make a new word. Write a sentence for each new word.

> sure   send

3. _____

4. _____

Name _____

Use the words in the box to complete the sentences.

| chore | porch | sport | roar | adore |

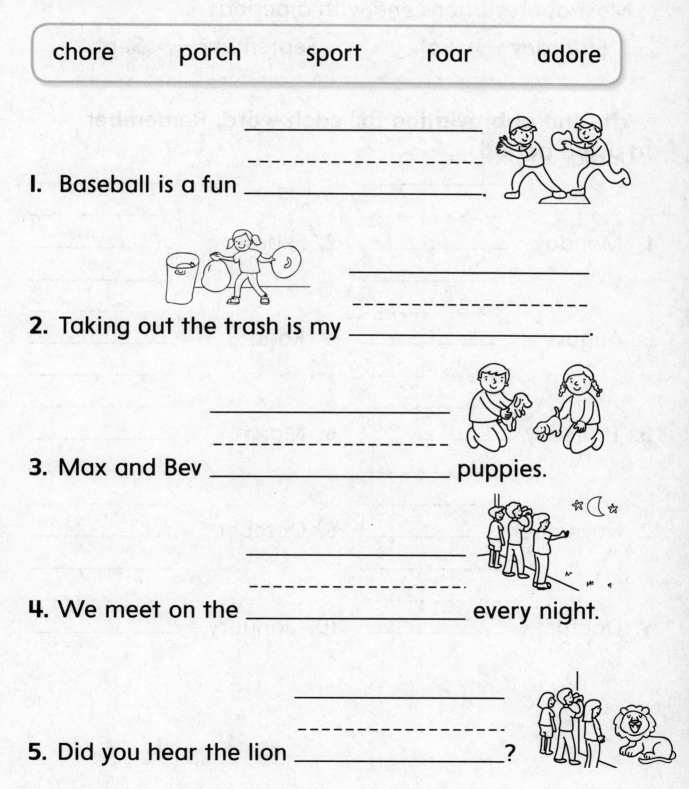

_____

- - - - - - - - - - - - - - - - - - -

1. Baseball is a fun _____.

_____

- - - - - - - - - - - - - - - - - - - -

2. Taking out the trash is my _____.

_____

- - - - - - - - - - - - - - - - - - -

3. Max and Bev _____ puppies.

_____

- - - - - - - - - - - - - - - - - - -

4. We meet on the _____ every night.

_____

- - - - - - - - - - - - - - - - - - -

5. Did you hear the lion _____?

Name _____

> An **abbreviation** is a short way of writing a word.
> Most abbreviations end with a period.
>
> Saturday ⟶ Sat.   September ⟶ Sept.

Write the abbreviation for each word. Remember to use a period.

1. Monday _____   2. February _____

3. August _____   4. Road _____

5. Thursday _____   6. March _____

7. November _____   8. October _____

9. Doctor _____   10. January _____

Name _____

In poems, some words that are close together all start with the same sound. This is called **alliteration**.

Sailor Sally sails across the sea.

Sometimes the words sound like what they tell about.

The whishing wind wheezed and whistled.

A. Read the sentences out loud. Circle words that begin with the same sound.

1. The bees buzz at the big brown bear.

2. Clang! Clatter! Cups crash and shatter.

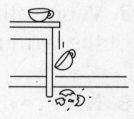

B. Say the words. Circle words that start with the same sound. Then use them to make a sentence.

3. cats   dot   can   back   catch

_____

- -

_____

4. hid   dogs   dig   good   down

_____

- -

_____

Name _____

A. Read the draft model. Use the questions to help you add more time-order words.

> ### Draft Model
>
> First, trains were invented and people could travel faster than horses. Cars were invented and people could go where they wanted faster, too. Planes were invented and people could travel across the ocean in just a few hours.

1. What is the topic of the writing?

2. What time-order word is used in the writing?

3. What other time-order words could be added to the writing?

B. Now revise the draft by adding time-order words to tell the order in which the events happened.

_____

- -

_____

_____

- -

_____

_____

- -

_____

Name _____

The letters <u>ou</u> and <u>ow</u> stand for the sounds you hear in the middle of **mouth** and **town**.

Circle the picture whose name has the same sounds you hear in the middle of <u>town</u>. Write <u>ou</u> or <u>ow</u> to complete the word that names the picture.

1. h _____ se

2. cr _____ n

3. br _____

4. m _____ se

5. cl _____ n

Name _____

Match each sentence to a picture.

1. Her socks are not the same **color**.

 a.

2. There is **nothing** left to eat.

 b.

3. It is too **early** to wake up.

 c.

4. He **thought** it might rain.

 d.

5. **Oh**, no! The dog is digging up the garden!

 e.

6. I want this hat **instead**.

 f.

Name _____

A. Write a sentence that uses the word <u>scrambled</u>. Then draw a picture to go with your sentence.

_____

- -

_____

B. Write a sentence that uses the word <u>suddenly</u>. Then draw a picture to go with your sentence.

_____

- -

_____

Name _____

Fill in the Problem and Solution Chart. Use words from the story.

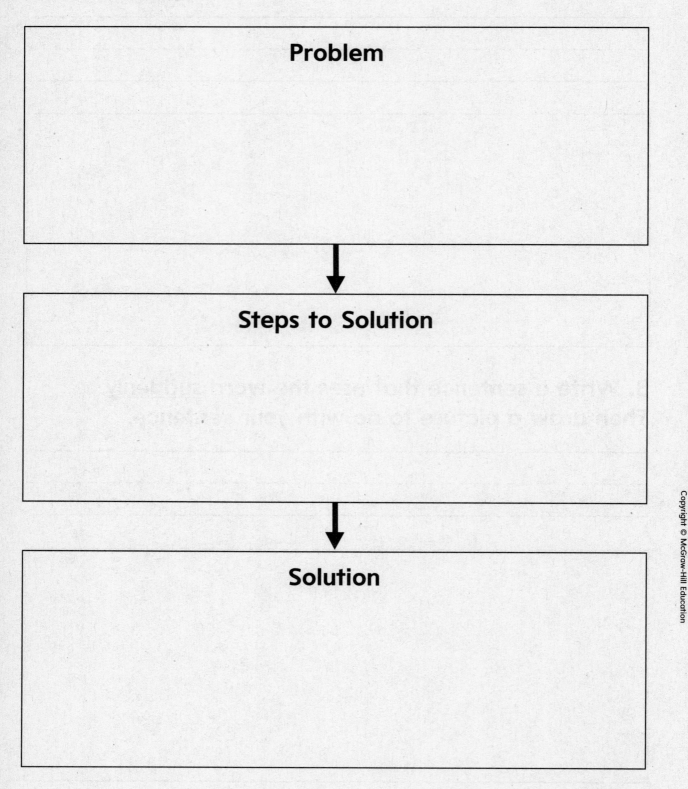

Problem

Steps to Solution

Solution

They played some more.
Then Dad said, "You can look now.
We are back at our brown house."
"That wasn't boring at all!" said
Howie.

④

Howie and Dad have a long
ride home.
"I do not like the bus ride," said
Howie.
"It is so boring."

Dad's Game

①

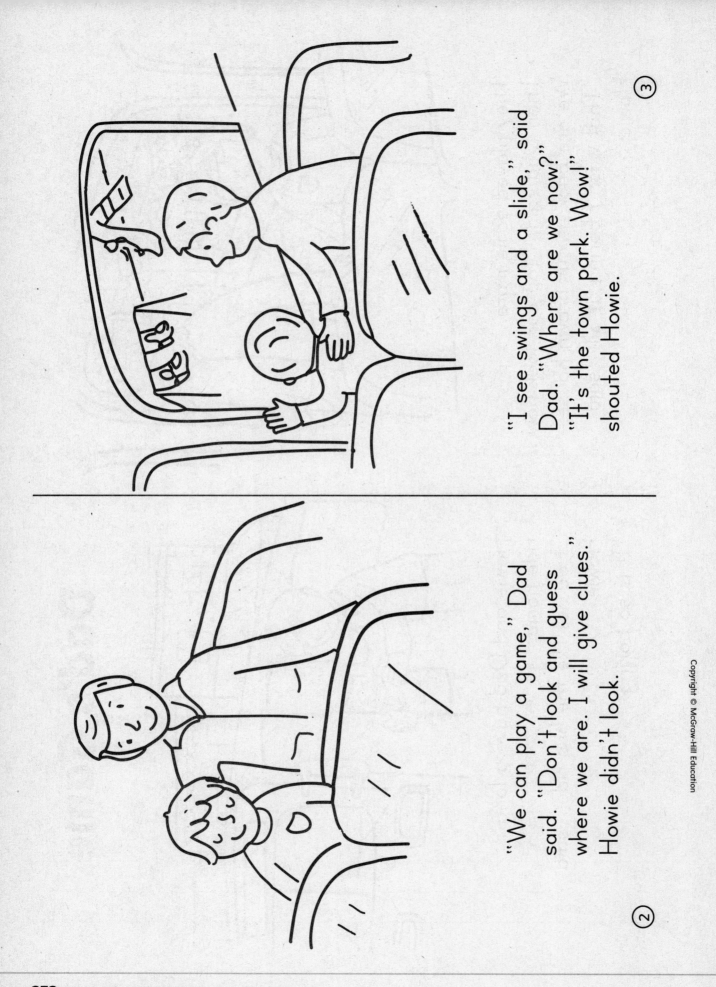

"I see swings and a slide," said Dad. "Where are we now?"
"It's the town park. Wow!" shouted Howie.

③

"We can play a game," Dad said. "Don't look and guess where we are. I will give clues." Howie didn't look.

②

Name _____

A. Reread "Dad's Game." Then write "problem," "step to a solution," or "solution" below each sentence.

I. Howie and Dad have a long ride home.

_____

- -

_____

2. Dad says, "We can play a game."

_____

- -

_____

3. "We are back at our brown house," said Dad.

_____

- -

_____

B. Work with a partner. Read the passage aloud. Pay attention to expression. Stop after one minute. Fill out the chart.

	Words Read	–	Number of Errors	=	Words Correct Score
First Read		–		=	
Second Read		–		=	

Name _____

A **suffix** is a word part added to the end of a word to make a new word.

The suffix **-or** means "a person who."
The suffix **-ful** means "full of."
The suffix **-less** means "without."
The suffix **-ly** means "in a way that is."

Read each sentence. Use the meaning of -or, -full, -less, or -ly as a clue to the meaning of the bold word. Match the sentence with the word's meaning.

1. The new puppy is **playful**.   in a way that's bold

2. Dad is a good **sailor**.   a person who visits

3. The glass of water is **colorless**.   full of play

4. Please be **careful** on the slide.   a person who sails

5. The hero sang **boldly**.   without color

6. There is a **visitor** at the door.   full of care

Name _____

Write the name of each picture. Then write a word from the box that rhymes with it.

| growl | grouch | mouse | plow | south | frown |

1. _____ _____

2. _____ _____

3. _____ _____

4. _____ _____

5. _____ _____

6. _____ _____

Name _____

Use the ending **-er** to compare two things:

    I am a **fast** runner. Min is **faster** than I am.

Use the ending **-est** to compare three or more things:

    I am a **fast** runner. Min is **faster** than I am.
    Pam is the **fastest** runner of all.

Add the ending -er or -est to the word in parentheses to complete the sentence.

1. This box is _____ than that one. (light)

2. Sam has the _____ desk in all of the class. (neat)

3. I am the _____ girl in my family. (old)

4. My dad is _____ than my mom. (short)

5. The sun is much _____ than the moon. (bright)

Name _____

> **Directions** tell you how to make or do something. A set of directions has two parts. The first part is a list of the materials you need. The second part tells the steps you need to follow.

A. Circle two materials that you need to make what is shown in each picture.

I. bread   nails   jam

2. stove   brushes   paints

3. sticks   snow   milk

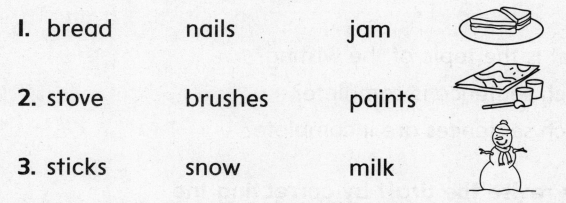

B. The steps to make toast are not in the right order. Number the steps to put them in order.

_____ Spread the toast with jam or butter.

_____ Get two slices of bread.

_____ Put the bread in the toaster.

_____ Wait for the bread to get brown.

Name _____

A. Read the draft model. Use the questions to help you correct the incomplete sentences.

> ## Draft Model
>
> A lot of different sounds at school! The bell rings when school starts and when school ends, and when it's time for lunch. Children at recess and in the halls, too.

I. What is the topic of the writing?

2. Which sentence is complete?

3. Which sentences are incomplete?

B. Now revise the draft by correcting the incomplete sentences.

_____

- -

_____

_____

- -

_____

_____

- -

_____

Name _____

> The letters **oi** and **oy** can stand for the sound you hear in the middle of **noise** and at the end of **joy**.

Use the words in the box to complete each sentence. Write the word on the line.

> enjoys   boil   Roy   toy   point   coin

_____

1. My name is _____.

_____

2. This _____ is a dime.

_____

3. She _____ painting.

_____

4. This is the baby's _____.

_____

5. The water will _____.

_____

6. That _____ is sharp!

Name _____

Write the word that completes each sentence.

| above | build | fall | knew | money | toward |

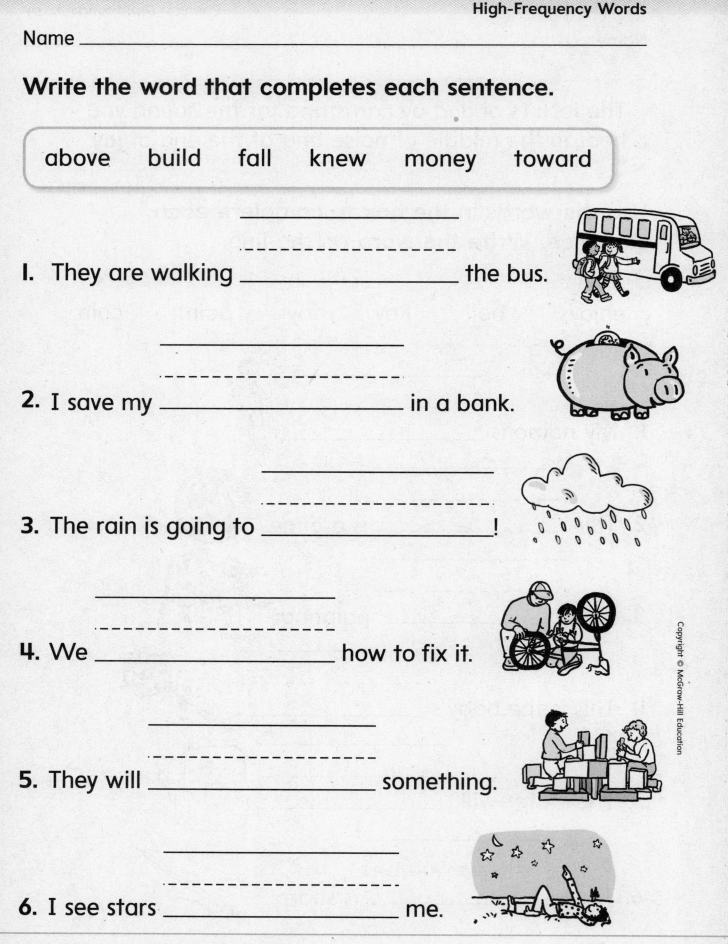

1. They are walking _____ the bus.

2. I save my _____ in a bank.

3. The rain is going to _____!

4. We _____ how to fix it.

5. They will _____ something.

6. I see stars _____ me.

Name _____

> **balance:** A thing can **<u>balance</u>** if it can stay in one place without falling.
>
> **section:** A <u>section</u> is a small part of something bigger.

Write a vocabulary word from the box to finish each sentence.

> balance   section

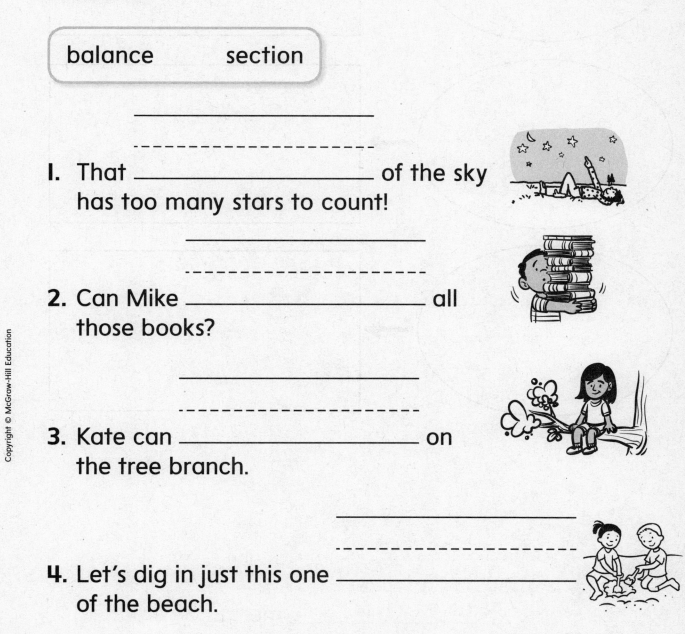

_____

\- - - - - - - - - - - - - - - - - - - -

1. That _____ of the sky has too many stars to count!

_____

\- - - - - - - - - - - - - - - - - - - -

2. Can Mike _____ all those books?

_____

\- - - - - - - - - - - - - - - - - - - -

3. Kate can _____ on the tree branch.

_____

\- - - - - - - - - - - - - - - - - - - -

4. Let's dig in just this one _____ of the beach.

Name _____

Fill in the Cause and Effect Chart. Use words from the story.

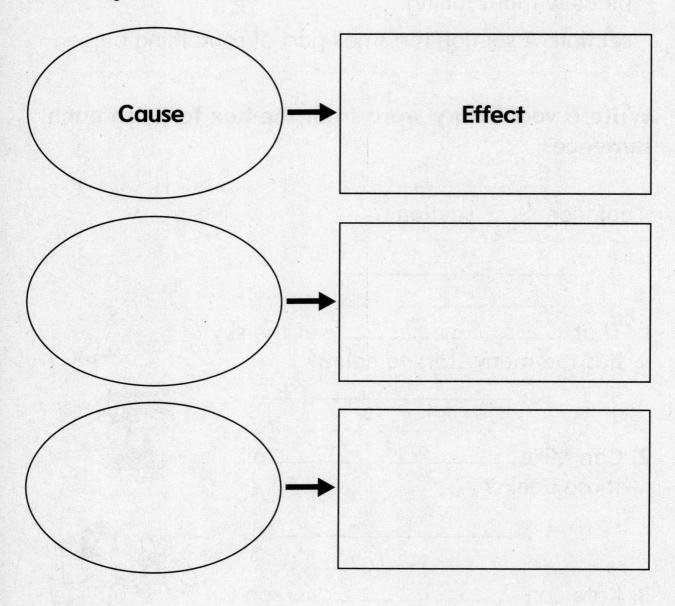

Cause → Effect

④

Next, make a head. Use stones or coins to make a face. Stick in branches for arms. Give him a hat and a pointy nose. Enjoy!

How to Build a Snowman

Look! Do you see wet, heavy snow fall from above? That means fun. You can build a snowman!

①

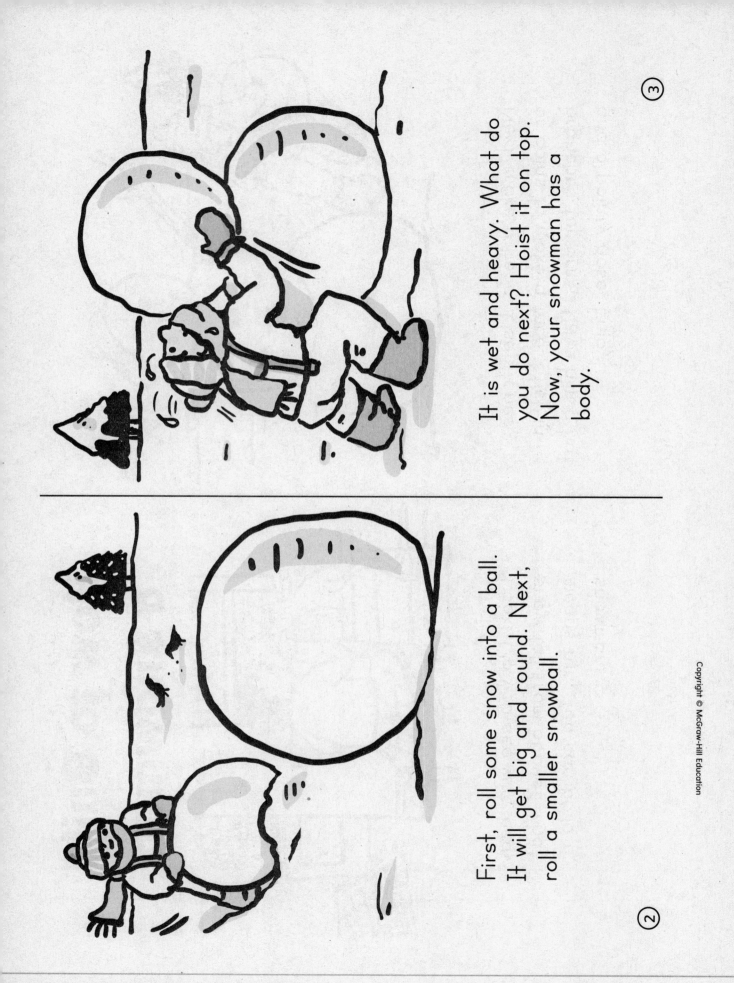

It is wet and heavy. What do you do next? Hoist it on top. Now, your snowman has a body.

③

First, roll some snow into a ball. It will get big and round. Next, roll a smaller snowball.

②

Name _____

A. Reread "How to Build a Snowman." Then read each cause. Choose the sentence below the cause that tells the effect. Circle it.

I. The snow falls.

Branches can be the arms.

You can build a snowman.

2. Roll some snow in a ball.

Snow falls from above.

It will get big and round.

3. Use stones or coins.

You can make arms.

You can make a face.

B. Work with a partner. Read the passage aloud. Pay attention to intonation and phrasing. Stop after one minute. Fill out the chart.

	Words Read	–	Number of Errors	=	Words Correct Score
First Read		–		=	
Second Read		–		=	

Name _____

An action word with the ending **-ed** means the action happened in the past.

An action word with the ending **-ing** means the action is happening now.

If you see a new word, look for the ending **-ed** or **-ing** and a root word. Use the meanings of the word parts to figure out the meaning of the new word.

A. Underline the ending. Circle the root word.

1. jumping

2. packed

3. pointing

4. cleaned

B. Write a sentence using a word above.

_____

5. _____

_____

_____

Name _____

Write <u>oi</u> or <u>oy</u> to complete each word. Then write the word.

1. _____ c o w b _____ _____

2. _____ p ___ n t _____

3. _____ b ___ l _____

4. _____ j _____ _____

5. _____ c ___ n _____

6. _____ t ___ s _____

Name _____

Many two-syllable words end with a **consonant** + <u>le</u>. The consonant + <u>le</u> always stay together in the last syllable.

tum/**ble** = tumble   sim/**ple** = simple

puz/**zle** = puzzle

Read the word. Draw a line between the syllables in each word. Write the two syllables.

_____ _____

1. handle _____ _____

_____ _____

2. crumble _____ _____

_____ _____

3. title _____ _____

_____ _____

4. bubble _____ _____

_____ _____

5. turtle _____ _____

_____ _____

6. sample _____ _____

Name _____

> **Captions** give readers more information about a photo or picture.

Circle the caption that tells about the picture.

1.

This is Newtown Bridge.

This is Newtown School.

2.

They are building a house.

They are building a park.

3.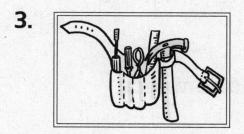

This hard hat keeps them safe.

This tool belt helps them carry tools.

4.

He is building a porch.

He is putting on a roof.

5.

The ship will travel far.

The bus takes you home.

6.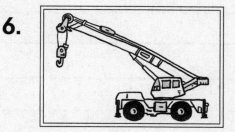

This small car goes fast.

This tall crane lifts things.

Name _____

A. Read the draft model. Use the questions to help you add a topic to the writing.

Draft Model

The outside can be made of bricks, wood or mud. Wood can be used to make floors, doors, and a roof, too. Glass is used for windows and sometimes even for the walls.

I. Does the writing tell what the topic is?

2. What do the sentences tell about?

3. What sentence could you add to tell what the topic is?

B. Now revise the draft by adding a sentence about the topic.

_____

_____

_____

_____

_____

_____

Name _____

> The letters **oo** can stand for the sound you hear in the middle of **moon**.
>
> The underlined letters in the words below show some other ways to spell the same sound.
>
> tr**u**th   bl**ue**   n**ew**   t**u**be   fr**ui**t   y**ou**

Read the first word. Then circle another word in the row with the same ending sounds.

I. **spoon**   sock   noon   both

2. **grew**   peg   goat   flew

3. **clue**   glue   call   nice

4. **Ruth**   scarf   pail   truth

5. **group**   game   soup   walk

Name _____

Complete each sentence. Use one of the words in the box.

| answer | brought | busy | door | enough | eyes |

_____

- - - - - - - - - - - - - - - - - -

1. Dad said, "Please _____ me now."

_____

- - - - - - - - - - - - - - - - - -

2. We use our _____ to see.

_____

- - - - - - - - - - - - - - - - - -

3. Gram _____ me a gift today.

_____

- - - - - - - - - - - - - - - - - -

4. Mom is too _____ to go to the park today.

_____

- - - - - - - - - - - - - - - - - -

5. Do we have _____ eggs to make the cupcakes?

_____

- - - - - - - - - - - - - - - - - -

6. Please close the _____ when you come in.

Name _____

demand: If you **demand** that someone do something, you ask forcefully or strongly.

emergency: An **emergency** is something unexpected that you need to take care of right away.

A. Match each sentence to the picture that it tells about.

1. The coaches demand that   a.
   their team works hard.

2. We learned what to do   b.
   in case of an emergency.

B. Complete each sentence. Use a word from the box.

| demand   emergency |

_____

3. I _____ that you listen to me!

4. You can use a flashlight in an _____.

Name _____

Fill in the Theme Chart. Use words from the story.

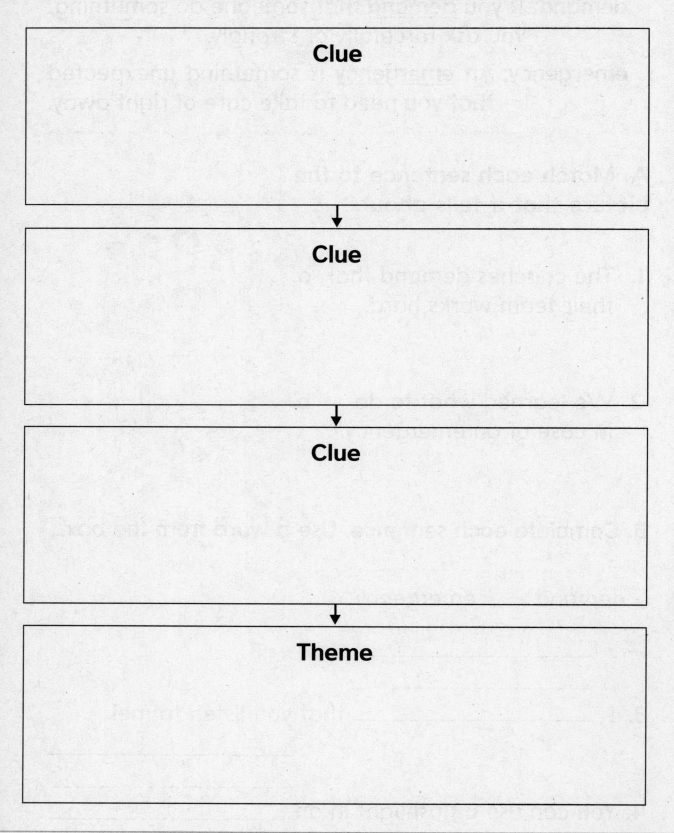

Clue

↓

Clue

↓

Clue

↓

Theme

Working Together

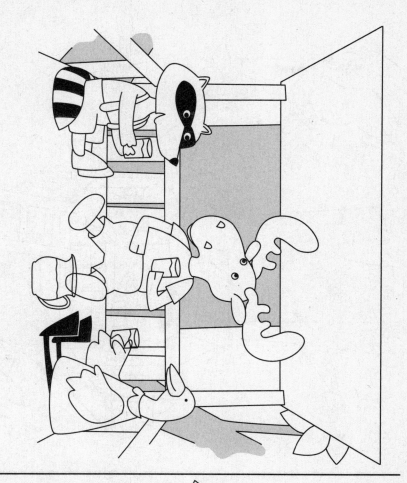

Raccoon was building a tree house. "This is the best tree house ever," he said. "But it's a lot of work. It is hard to do alone."

①

The pals drank cool water. Soon, the tree house was done. "I couldn't have done it without my new pals!" said Raccoon.

④

Next, Goose flew by. "What a great tree house!" she said. "I can help. I will get cool water for you to drink."

③

Just then, Moose came by. "I can help you," he said. "I even have my tools. We can work together."

②

Name _____

A. Reread "Working Together."
Match each clue to the picture it tells about.

1. Raccoon needs help.

a.

2. Moose has tools.

b.

3. Goose will get cool water.

c.

4. What is the theme of the story? Use the clues
   to help you.

_____

- -

_____

B. Work with a partner. Read the passage aloud.
Pay attention to expression. Stop after one minute.
Fill out the chart.

	Words Read	–	Number of Errors	=	Words Correct Score
First Read		–		=	
Second Read		–		=	

Name _____

> **Synonyms** are words with the same or almost the same meaning.
>
> Some synonyms for **happy** are **glad** and **joyful**.

A. Circle the two words that have the same or almost the same meaning.

I. sparkle   glow   funny

2. shout   found   yell

3. busy   build   make

4. angry   happy   mad

5. none   cold   chilly

6. twirl   spin   grab

B. Write a sentence using a word you circled above.

7. _____

_____

Name

Read the word. Circle the letters that make the sound you hear at the end of <u>too</u>. Then circle the picture that the word names.

I. roof

2. flute

3. screw

4. fruit

5. soup

Name _____

> A **suffix** is a word part you can add to the end of
> a word to change its meaning.
>
> The suffix **-ful** means **full** or **full of**.
> The word **help<u>ful</u>** means **full of help**.
>
> The suffix **-<u>less</u>** means **without**.
> The word **help<u>less</u>** means **without help**.

Circle the suffix in each word.

1. useless

2. joyful

3. fearless

4. painless

5. hopeful

6. useful

7. senseless

8. fearful

9. painful

10. pointless

Name _____

> A **caption** tells more about a photograph or picture.

A. Look at the picture. Read the caption. Answer the questions.

The Bakers clean up Green Park.

_____

- -

1. Who are the people in _____
the picture? _____

- -

2. Where are the people? _____

B. Look at the picture. Read the caption. Answer the questions.

Jane Tate told the class
about taking care of trees.

_____

- -

3. Who is the woman in the picture?_____

_____

- -

4. What is she doing? _____

- -

_____

Name _____

A. Read the draft model. Use the questions to help you vary the length of the sentences.

> ### Draft Model
>
> We help the earth. We recycle bottles. We pick up trash.

1. What is the topic of the writing?

2. Are there some long and some short sentences?

3. How can you make the lengths of some sentences different?

B. Now revise the draft by varying the length of the sentences.

_____

_____

_____

_____

_____

_____

Name _____

Say **paw**. The same vowel sound can be spelled with **a** as in **m**a**ll**, **au** as in **f**au**lt**, **augh** as in **t**augh**t**, and **al** as in **t**al**k**.

Write the words from the box that have the same sound-spelling as the name of the picture.

stalk	taught	fall	haul	claw
small	chalk	cause	paw	naughty

I. crawl

_____   _____

_____   _____

2. call

_____   _____

_____   _____

3. sauce

_____   _____

_____   _____

4. caught

_____   _____

_____   _____

5. walk

_____   _____

_____   _____

Name _____

A. Complete each sentence. Use one of the words in the box.

brother	father	friend	love	mother	picture

1. My _____ Liz goes to my school.

2. I _____ to run around the park.

3. I smiled for my class _____.

4. My _____ and _____ tell me to go to bed.

5. Paul's _____ is the same age as I am.

B. Write your own sentence using a word from the box.

6. _____

Name _____

> When you **accept** something, you take it or agree to it.
> If you do something **often**, you do it a lot.

A. Use a vocabulary word from the box to finish each sentence.

> accept   often

_____
- - - - - - - - - - - - - - - - - -

1. Chris visits the park _____ to ride his bike.

_____
- - - - - - - - - - - - - - - - - -

2. Kyle was ready to _____ the award from the mayor.

B. Choose one of the vocabulary words from the box above. Write a sentence of your own. Then draw a picture to go with your sentence.

_____
- -

3. _____

Name _____

Fill in the Author's Purpose Chart. Use details from the story.

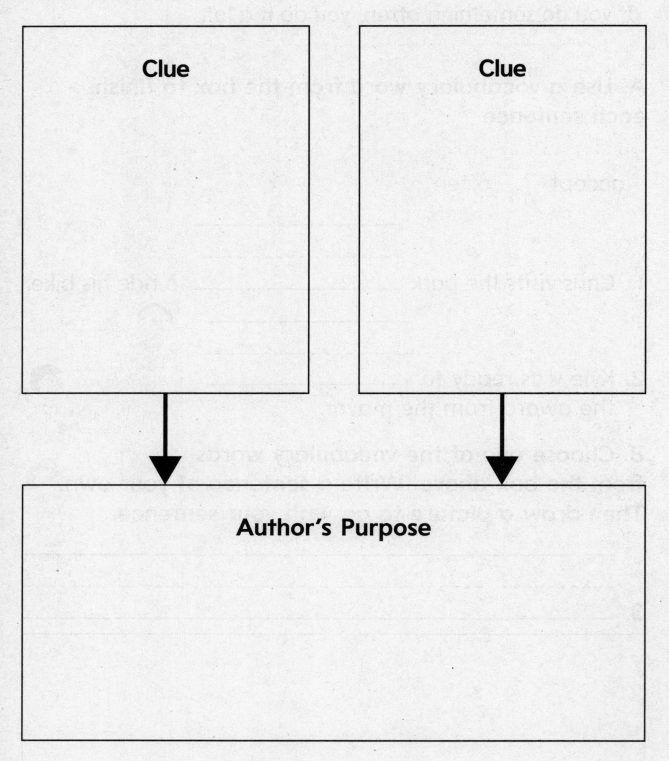

Clue

Clue

Author's Purpose

(4)

Coaches love to play, teach, and talk about their sport. They help us love it, too!

Coaches

Coaches help us learn to play a sport. First, they teach the rules of the sport. That way the players know the game.

(1)

③

Coaches also help the players work together. They teach players to all get along and to share. That's because this helps make a good team.

Coaches help players in lots of ways. They show players how to throw and hit the ball. They train players to run fast.

②

Name _____

A. Read the story and follow the directions.

I. Why did the author write "Coaches"? Choose the best answer.

ⓐ to tell what coaches do

ⓑ to tell about sports

ⓒ to tell about how to play soccer

2. Write words from the story that tell you what coaches show players.

_____ _____ _____

------------- ------------- -------------

_____ _____ _____

3. What makes a good team? Choose the best answer.

ⓐ They do not work hard.

ⓑ They like to lose.

ⓒ They work together.

B. Work with a partner. Read the passage aloud. Pay attention to intonation. Stop after one minute. Fill out the chart.

	Words Read	–	Number of Errors	=	Words Correct Score
First Read		–		=	
Second Read		–		=	

Name _____

> Words with opposite meanings are called **antonyms**.

Read each sentence. Circle the word that has the opposite meaning of the bold word.

1. The **tiny** mouse ran away.

   small   cute   huge

2. Jimmy felt **better** after a day in bed.

   worse   happy   best

3. Melissa told us the show was **great**.

   long   awful   good

4. The ride was very **loud**.

   wild   noisy   quiet

5. Paul **always** plays baseball on Fridays.

   faster   often   never

6. Dad can climb the **tall** ladder.

   short   safe   big

Name _____

Use the letters <u>a</u>, <u>aw</u>, <u>au</u>, <u>augh</u>, or <u>al</u> to complete each word. Write the letters on the line.

1. c l _____ _____

2. t _____ t

3. b _____ l l

4. c _____ t

5. h _____ l

6. t _____ k

7. y _____ n

Name _____

> **Vowel teams** are formed by two letters in a word that stand for one vowel sound. The underlined letters in these words are examples of vowel teams.
>
> h<u>ea</u>t   h<u>oo</u>d   st<u>ay</u>   <u>ou</u>t   b<u>oy</u>   s<u>aw</u>
>
> Vowel teams stay together in the same syllable.
>
> <u>oa</u>t/m<u>ea</u>l   r<u>ow</u>/ing

Underline the vowel teams in each word. Draw a line between the syllables.

1. drawing

2. neatest

3. playground

4. mailbox

5. peeling

6. growing

7. raincoat

8. cowboy

9. bookcase

10. sixteen

Name _____

> Sensory words tell what something looks, smells, feels, tastes, or sounds like.
>
> The **fluffy white** clouds float in the sky.

Circle the sensory word a writer could use to tell about each picture.

1.   sleepy   loud   tiny

2.   fast   sweet   noisy

3.   wet   dry   pink

4.   sunny   stormy   quiet

5.   dark   hot   icy

6.   yummy   hairy   cold

Name _____

A. Read the draft model. Use the questions to help you use your own voice in the writing.

> ### Draft Model
>
> Mom helps me and takes care of me. She reads me books every night. She makes my lunch every day.

1. What is the topic of the writing?

2. Does the writer use his or her own voice to tell how they feel?

3. How can you add your own voice to the writing?

B. Now revise the draft by telling how you feel about the topic.

Name _____

When you see **wr**, **kn**, **gn** at the beginning of a word or syllable, the first letter is silent.

w̲rap   k̲nit   g̲naw

A. Circle the word that names each picture.

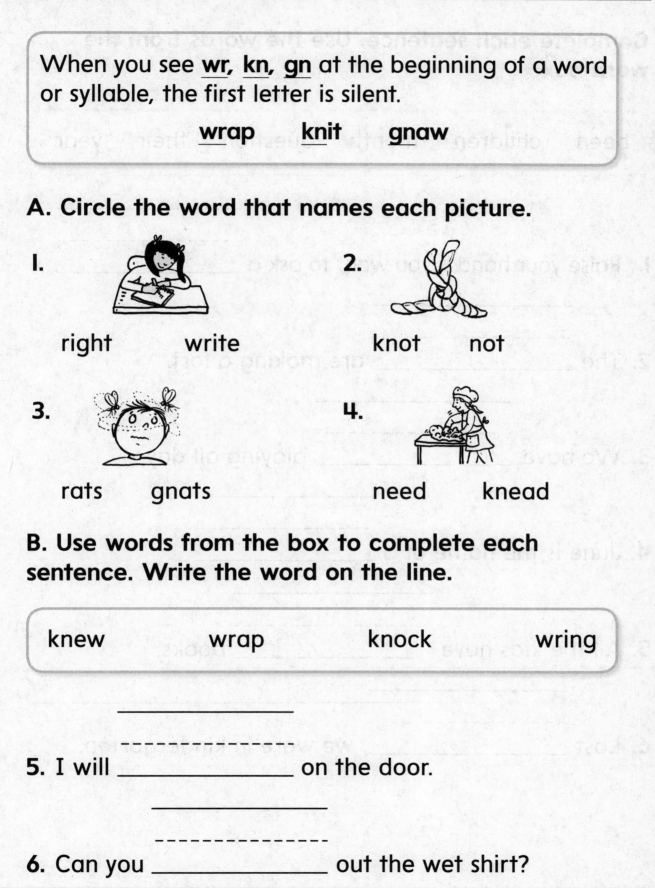

I.

right   write

2.

knot   not

3.

rats   gnats

4.

need   knead

B. Use words from the box to complete each sentence. Write the word on the line.

knew	wrap	knock	wring

_____

5. I will _____ on the door.

_____

6. Can you _____ out the wet shirt?

Name _____

Complete each sentence. Use the words from the word box.

> been   children   month   question   their   year

1. Raise your hand if you want to ask a _____.

2. The _____ are making a fort.

3. We have _____ playing all day.

4. June is the name of a _____.

5. All the kids have _____ books.

6. Last _____, we were in kindergarten.

Name _____

A **country** is a land where a group of people live.

　We live in a <u>country</u> called the United States.

When a person **gathers** things, the things are put in the same place.

　Sam <u>gathers</u> the mugs.

Write <u>country</u> or <u>gathers</u> to complete each sentence.

1. Spain is a _____ .

2. Mr. Jones _____ our papers.

3. We went to a _____ called France.

4. Ana _____ wood for a fire.

Name _____

Fill in the Cause and Effect Chart. Use details from the story.

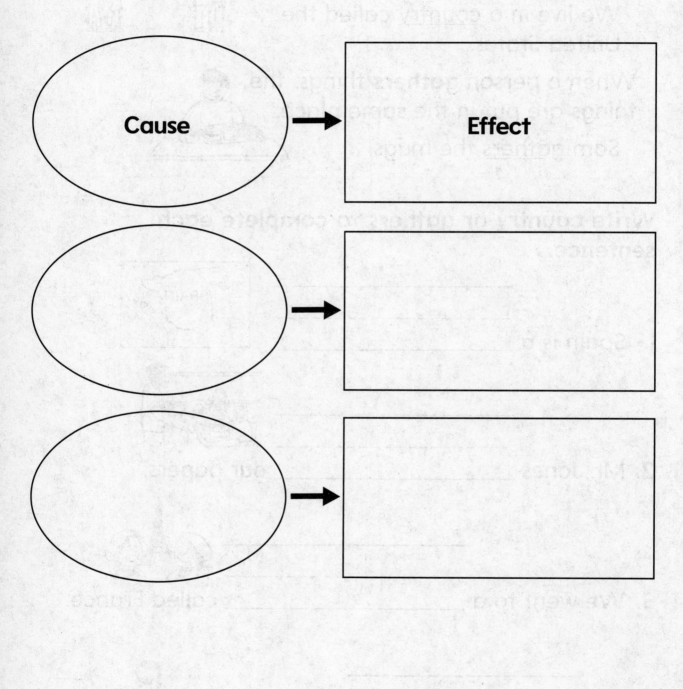

Cause → **Effect**

Storm Watch

"A big storm is coming," Mom said. "We need to get ready." Paul was worried. He did not like storms. They can wreck things.

Paul wanted his blanket. He said, "We will need to stay warm." Dad got a phone. "I know we'll be ready," said Dad.

④

①

"I will write a list," said Paul.
Paul wrote the word "flashlight."
"We will need light," said Paul.
"In a storm, power can go out."

③

"There is time to plan," said Dad.
"We have to find all the things
we may need. We will need to
stay inside."

②

Name _____

A. Reread "Storm Watch." Then write "cause" or "effect" next to each sentence.

_____

- - - - - - - - - - - - -

1. A big storm is coming. _____ _____

- - - - - - - - - - - - -

2. Paul, his mom, and his dad make a plan. _____

_____

- - - - - - - - - - - - -

3. The house may get cold. _____

_____

- - - - - - - - - - - - -

4. Paul wants his blanket. _____

5. Paul and his parents gather the things they will need.

_____

- - - - - - - - - - - - -

_____

B. Work with a partner. Read the passage aloud. Pay attention to intonation. Stop after one minute. Fill out the chart.

	Words Read	–	Number of Errors	=	Words Correct Score
First Read		–		=	
Second Read		–		=	

Name _____

> Writers can use **similes** to help readers picture details. A simile compares one thing to another using the words <u>like</u> or <u>as</u>.
>
> The puddle is <u>as</u> big <u>as</u> a lake.
>
> The wind felt <u>like</u> an ice cube.

A. Read each sentence. Underline the words <u>like</u> or <u>as</u>. Circle the two things that are compared.

1. The storm was like a roller coaster.

2. The house is as dark as a cave.

3. The flashlight is like the sun.

4. The blanket is as warm as a bath.

5. Paul's list is as long as a book.

B. Choose a sentence above. Draw a picture of it.

Name _____

Write the word that completes each sentence. Use the words from the word box.

| gnat | wring | kneel | knew | wrap |

_____

- - - - - - - - - - - - - - - -

1. Dad _____ I wanted new shoes.

_____

- - - - - - - - - - - - - - - -

2. Nate does not like the _____.

_____

- - - - - - - - - - - - - - - -

3. Mom likes to _____ presents.

_____

- - - - - - - - - - - - - - - -

4. I will _____ the wet sheets.

_____

- - - - - - - - - - - - - - - -

5. We _____ on the floor.

Name _____

> A **compound word** is a word made up of two smaller words.
>
> ant + hill = anthill

A. Read each compound word. Write the two smaller words you see in each word.

_____   _____

1. raindrop   _____   _____

2. rowboat   _____   _____

3. afternoon   _____   _____

4. outside   _____   _____

B. Write a sentence using one or two compound words above.

5. _____

_____

Name _____

> A reading selection can have many sections.
> **Headings** tell what each section is about.

A. Read the selection about hot weather.

Beat the Heat!

Many people like hot weather. You can have fun on a hot day. But you must be careful.

The Sun on Your Skin

The sun can harm you. Wear a hat and put on sunscreen. Put on more sunscreen after you swim.

The Sun and Your Body

Make sure you drink lots of water. You need more water on a hot day.

B. Answer the questions about the selection.

I. What is one tip from the section with the heading "The Sun on Your Skin"?

wear a hat   drink lots of water

2. What is the last section about?

The Sun on Your Skin   The Sun and Your Body

Name _____

A. Read the draft model. Use the questions to help you add a main idea to the writing.

> ## Draft Model
>
> We like to work together and build a snowman. We have fun when we throw snow balls. We have even more fun when we go sledding down the big hill!

1. What is the topic of the writing?

2. What is the main idea? Is the main idea stated in the writing?

3. What sentence could you add to tell the main idea of the writing?

B. Now revise the draft by adding a sentence to tell the main idea.

_____
- -
_____
- -
_____
- -
_____
- -
_____

Name _____

> Sometimes three consonants form a **blend**.
>
> <u>scr</u>ap   <u>spl</u>ash   <u>spr</u>ay   <u>str</u>eet   <u>thr</u>ee   <u>shr</u>ub

Read the first word. Then circle another word in the line with the same three-letter blend.

1. **street**   straw   tree   sharp

2. **shrub**   shred   should   both

3. **scrap**   cry   scratch   school

4. **three**   thing   threw   tree

5. **spray**   spot   soap   spring

6. **splash**   seat   play   split

Name _____

Complete each sentence. Use one of the words in the box.

before	front	heard	push	tomorrow	your

1. Let's wash up _____ we eat lunch.

2. Is this _____ book or mine?

3. I helped Mom paint the _____ door.

4. We _____ the thunder.

5. Will you _____ me on the swing?

6. I have art class today and soccer _____.

Name _____

> **difficult:** Something that is **difficult** is not easy.
>
> **nobody:** **Nobody** means "no person."

Complete each sentence with a word from the word box. You will use each word two times.

> difficult   nobody

_____
- - - - - - - - - - - - - -

I. Riding a bike can be _____ for some and easy for others.

_____
- - - - - - - - - - - - - -

2. I heard a knock at the door, but _____ was there.

_____
- - - - - - - - - - - - - -

3. Do you think it is more _____ to make a kite or to fly it?

4. Mrs. Lu asked if anyone lost a notebook,

_____
- - - - - - - - - - - - - -

but _____ spoke up.

Name _____

Fill in the Theme Chart. Use words from the story.

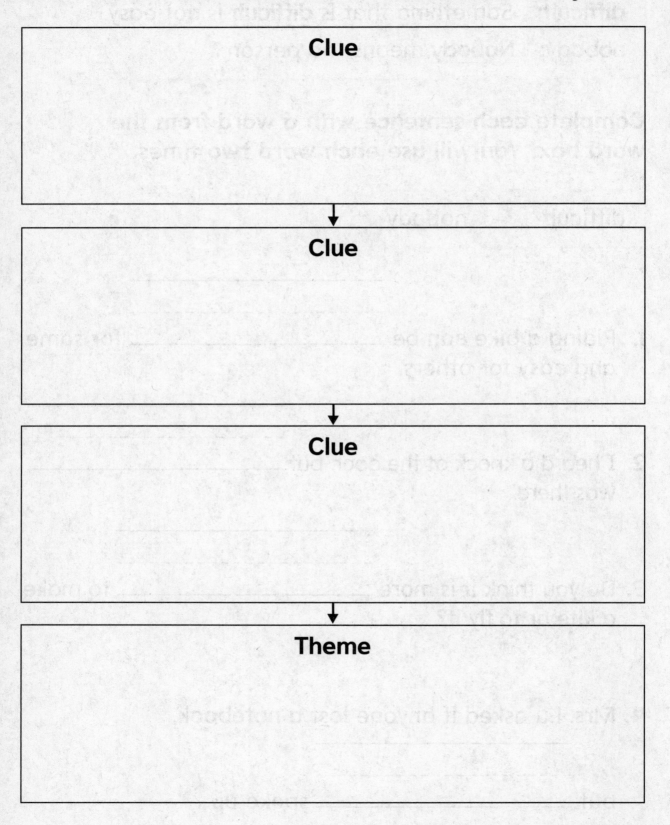

Clue

↓

Clue

↓

Clue

↓

Theme

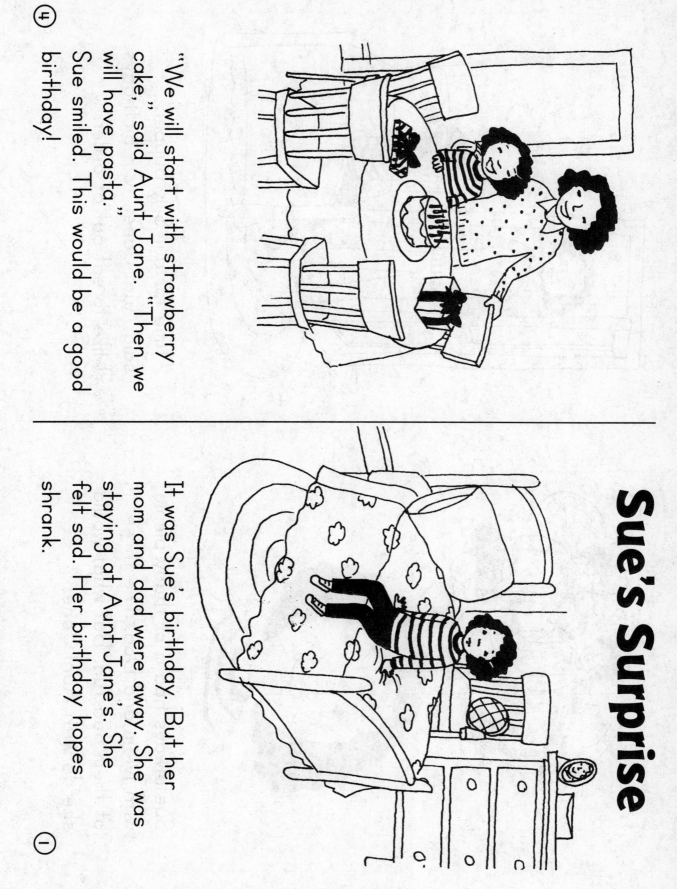

Sue's Surprise

It was Sue's birthday. But her mom and dad were away. She was staying at Aunt Jane's. She felt sad. Her birthday hopes shrank.

①

"We will start with strawberry cake," said Aunt Jane. "Then we will have pasta." Sue smiled. This would be a good birthday!

④

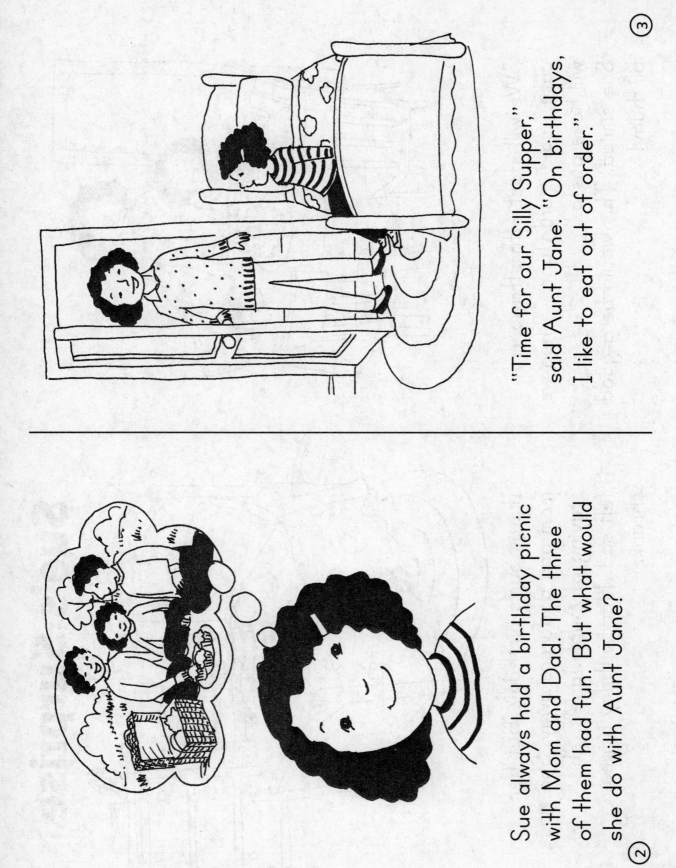

"Time for our Silly Supper,"
said Aunt Jane. "On birthdays,
I like to eat out of order."

③

Sue always had a birthday picnic
with Mom and Dad. The three
of them had fun. But what would
she do with Aunt Jane?

②

Name _____

A. Reread "Sue's Surprise." Match each story clue to the picture it tells about.

1. Sue was sad that her mom and dad were away.

a.

2. Sue always had a picnic with Mom and Dad.

b.

3. "Time for our Silly Supper," said Aunt Jane.

c.

4. What is the theme of the story? Use the clues to help you.

_____

- -

_____

B. Work with a partner. Read the passage aloud. Pay attention to phrasing. Stop after one minute. Fill out the chart.

	Words Read	–	Number of Errors	=	Words Correct Score
First Read		–		=	
Second Read		–		=	

Name _____

> A **compound word** is a longer word made up of two smaller words.
>
> The word **birdhouse** is a compound word.
>
> bird + house = birdhouse
>
> A **birdhouse** is a house for birds to live in.

A. Draw a line between the two smaller words in each compound word. Use the two words to help you match the compound word to its meaning.

1. toolbox   a bag t o carry books

2. snowball   a box to carry tools

3. toothbrush   a ball made of snow

4. bookbag   a brush to clean teeth

B. Write a sentence using a compound word above.

_____

- -

5. _____

_____

- -

_____

Name _____

Write the word on the line. Draw a line from the word to the picture it names.

I. thr + ee =

_____

- - - - - - - - - - - - - - - - - -

_____

a.

2. str + ing =

_____

- - - - - - - - - - - - - - - - - -

_____

b.

3. scr + atch =

_____

- - - - - - - - - - - - - - - - - -

_____

c.

4. spr + ay =

_____

- - - - - - - - - - - - - - - - - -

_____

d.

5. spl + it =

_____

- - - - - - - - - - - - - - - - - -

_____

e.

Name _____

Add **-ed** to an action word to tell what happened in the past.

Add **-ing** to tell what is happening now.

Change some words before adding **-ed** or **-ing**.

race – e + ed = raced   try – y + i + ed = tried

drop + p + ing = dropping

Complete each sentence. Add -ed or -ing to the word in parentheses. Write the new word.

_____

- - - - - - - - - - - - - - - - - -

1. I _____ the dog after his bath. (dry)

_____

- - - - - - - - - - - - - - - - - -

2. Who is _____ at the door now? (knock)

_____

- - - - - - - - - - - - - - - - - -

3. My cat _____ me yesterday. (scratch)

_____

- - - - - - - - - - - - - - - - - -

4. The bus _____ here last week. (stop)

_____

- - - - - - - - - - - - - - - - - -

5. Mom is _____ a letter. (write)

Name _____

> **Directions** are a list of steps that tell how to make or do something.

Read the directions. Answer the questions.

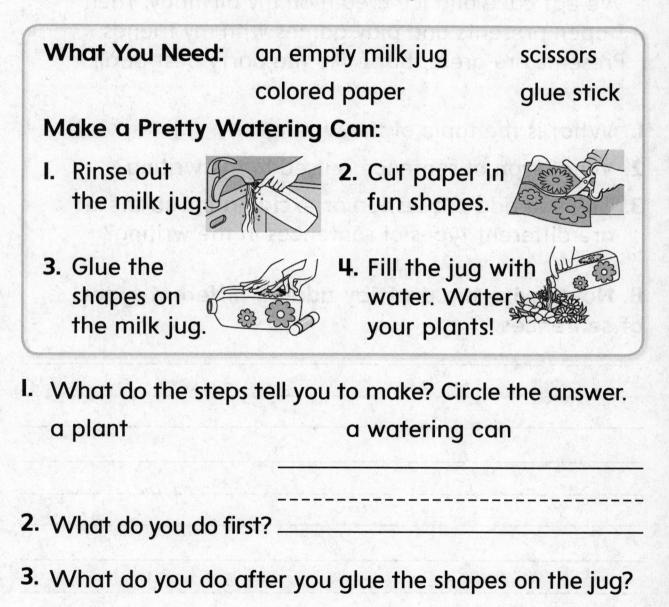

What You Need: an empty milk jug   scissors

colored paper   glue stick

Make a Pretty Watering Can:

1. Rinse out the milk jug.

2. Cut paper in fun shapes.

3. Glue the shapes on the milk jug.

4. Fill the jug with water. Water your plants!

1. What do the steps tell you to make? Circle the answer.

a plant   a watering can

_____

_____

2. What do you do first? _____

3. What do you do after you glue the shapes on the jug?

_____

_____

_____

Name _____

A. Read the draft model. Use the questions to help you use different types of sentences.

> ### Draft Model
> We eat cake and ice cream on my birthday. Then I open presents and play games with my friends. Presents are great, but I like the party best of all.

I. What is the topic of the writing?

2. What type of sentence is used in the writing?

3. Can you add a question or exclamation so there are different types of sentences in the writing?

B. Now revise the draft by adding different types of sentences.

_____
_____
_____
_____
_____

Name _____

> The letters **air** together can make the sound you hear at the end of **chair**.
>
> The letters **are** and **ear** can also make the same sound, as in **share** and **pear**.

Circle the word that completes the sentence. Then write the word.

_____

-----------------------.

1. My room is at the top of the _____.

   stairs   stars

_____

-----------------------.

2. Ruth has long _____.

   heat   hair

_____

-----------------------.

3. The noise might _____ you.

   scarf   scare

_____

-----------------------.

4. I think I will _____ a big coat today.

   wrote   wear

Name _____

Complete each sentence. Use one of the words in the box.

| favorite   few   gone   surprise   wonder   young |

_____
\- -

1. I like grapes, but pears are my _____ food.

_____
\- - - - - - - - - - - - - - - - - - -

2. Spot is a very _____ puppy.

_____
\- - - - - - - - - - - - - - - - - - -

3. It will be fun to _____ Mom when she comes home.

_____
\- - - - - - - - - - - - - - - - - - -

4. There are only a _____ books on my shelf.

_____
\- - - - - - - - - - - - - - - - - - -

5. I _____ what time Dad's plane will land.

6. Mom made cupcakes, but now they are all

_____
\- - - - - - - - - - - - - - - - - - -
_____.

Name _____

> **nation:** A **nation** is a group of people living in one
> country.
>
> **unite:** To **unite** is to join together.

A. Write unite or nation to finish each sentence. Circle the picture that best matches the sentence.

1. This is the flag for our _____.

a.   b.

2. Our class will _____ with Mr. Tate's
   class to see the play.

a.   b.

B. Match the word to its meaning.

3. unite   a. a group of people
                                     living in one country

4. nation   b. to join together

Name _____

Fill in the Author's Purpose Chart. Use words from the story.

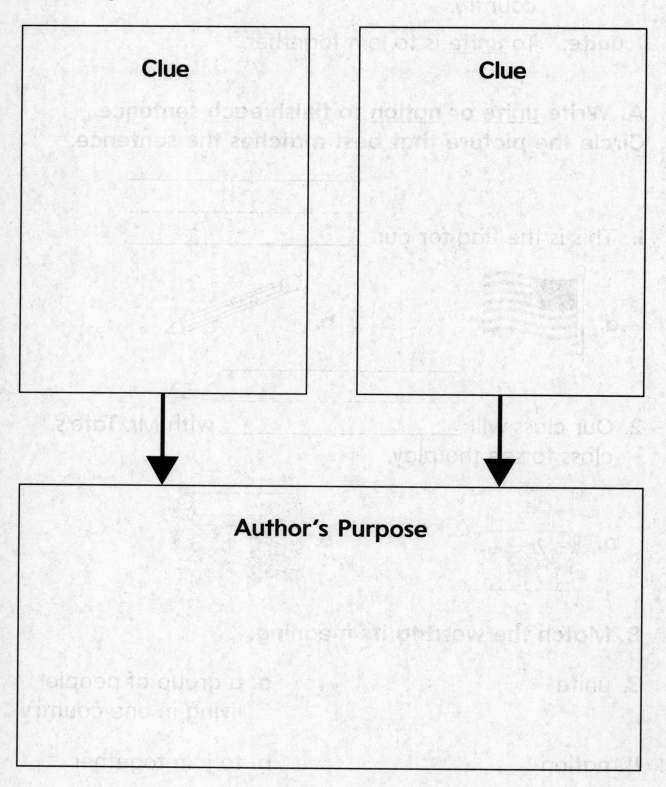

Favorite Days

Do you have a favorite day of the year? There are many special days. We celebrate each in special ways.

①

Birthdays are favorite days to share, too. Many young children have parties and wear a hat. What is your favorite day?

④

Mother's Day is in May. Father's Day is in June. Children take care to do something special for their moms and dads.

③

New Year's Day is the first day of the year. Some families stay home and play games together. They wonder what the new year will be like.

②

Name _____

A. Read the sentences from "Favorite Days."
Fill in the circle next to the correct answer.

I. New Year's Day is the first day of the year.
The author's purpose is to

○ tell how children love to play games.

○ tell about New Year's Day.

2. Father's Day is in June. The author's purpose is to

○ tell about Father's Day.

○ tell how to make a Father's Day card.

B. Why did the author write "Favorite Days"? Write a sentence.

_____

- -

3. _____

C. Work with a partner. Read the passage aloud.
Pay attention to phrasing. Stop after one minute.
Fill out the chart.

	Words Read	–	Number of Errors	=	Words Correct Score
First Read		–		=	
Second Read		–		=	

Name _____

> Writers can use **metaphors** to help readers picture details. A metaphor compares one thing to another.
>
> The snow is a big white blanket.
>
> Unlike a simile, a metaphor does not use <u>like</u> or <u>as</u>.

A. Read each sentence. Look at the underlined words. Then circle the sentence that tells how the two things are alike.

I. The <u>rainbow</u> is a <u>box of crayons</u> spilled from the clouds.

Both have lots of colors.   Both are in a box.

2. The <u>cloud</u> is <u>cotton candy</u> floating by.

Both are in the sky.   Both are fluffy.

3. The <u>oven</u> is a <u>dragon that breathes fire</u>.

Both have heat inside.   Both are very soft.

B. Circle the word that best completes the sentence. Write the word on the line.

4. Thunder is a _____.

bell   whistle   drum

Name _____

Read the word. Circle the letters that make the sound you hear at the end of ch<u>air</u>. Circle the picture that the word names.

1. pear

2. hair

3. square

4. bear

5. stairs

Name _____

> Some words have more than one syllable.
>
> When a word has a vowel followed by **r**, the vowel and **r** stay in the same syllable.
>
> turtle = **tur** / tle   circus = **cir** / cus
> target = **tar** / get   story = st**or** / y

Read the words. Make a check mark √ next to the word that has a vowel followed by r. Draw a line between the syllables in that word.

I. _____ turkey   _____ rocky

2. _____ rabbit   _____ market

3. _____ perfect   _____ pencil

4. _____ frozen   _____ forty

5. _____ thirteen   _____ ticket

Name _____

Look at the map. Then answer the questions.

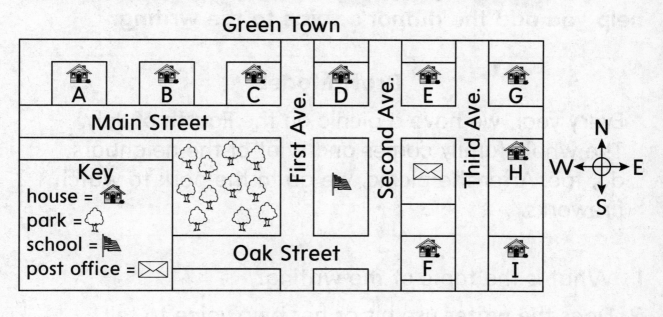

1. How many houses are in Green Town? _____

2. How many schools are in Green Town? _____

3. If you lived in house A, what street would you walk on to get to the park?

    _____

    -

4. If you lived in house H, what street would you cross to get to the post office?

    _____

    -

Name _____

A. Read the draft model. Use the questions to help you add the author's voice to the writing.

> ### Draft Model
> Every year, we have a picnic on the Fourth of July. The whole family comes and a lot of the neighbors do, too. After the picnic, we go to the park to watch fireworks.

I. What is the topic of the writing?

2. Does the writer use his or her own voice to tell about the picnic?

3. How can you add the writer's voice to the writing?

B. Now revise the draft by telling how the writer might feel about the topic.

_____

- -

_____

- -

_____

- -

_____